Death by Rock 'n' Roll

Death by Rock 'n' Roll

The Untimely Deaths of the Legends of Rock

by Gary J. Katz

A Citadel Press Book
Published by Carol Publishing Group

A Citadel Press Book
Published by Carol Publishing Group
Citadel Press is a registered trademark of Carol Communications, Inc.
Editorial Offices: 600 Madison Avenue, New York, N.Y. 10022
Sales and Distribution Offices: 120 Enterprise Avenue, Secaucus, N.J. 07094
In Canada: Canadian Manda Group, P.O. Box 920, Station U, Toronto, Ontario
    M8Z 5P9
Queries regarding rights and permissions should be addressed to
Carol Publishing Group, 600 Madison Avenue, New York, N.Y. 10022

Carol Publishing Group books are available at special discounts for bulk purchases,
sales promotions, fund-raising, or educational purposes. Special editions can be
created to specifications. For details, contact Special Sales Department,
Carol Publishing Group, 120 Enterprise Avenue, Secaucus, N.J. 07094

Manufactured in the United States of America

10 9 8 7 6 5 4 3 2 1

Library of Congress Cataloging-in-Publication Data
Katz, Gary J.
    Death by rock 'n' roll : the untimely deaths of the legends of
rock / by Gary J. Katz.
        p.   cm.
    "A Citadel Press book."
    ISBN 0-8065-1581-3 (pbk.)
    1. Rock musicians—Mortality.   I. Title.
ML3534.K37   1994
781.66'092'2—dc20   94-19224
                                                            CIP
                                                            MN

To my lovely wife, Sheryl, and my two beautiful girls, Jessica and Christina. Their support made this book a reality.

A special thanks to my parents, Theodore and Molly, who have been involved in all my adventures.

I would also like to thank the following people for their help and support:

Sam Houston Andrew III
Joey and Kathie Molland
Dave & Christine Pegg
Barriemore Barlow
Tony Grafasi
Bill Curbishley
Carl Depolo
Ken Ciabatti
Ralph Cooper
Harry Maslin
Richard Lush
Mike Gibbins
Harvey Brooks
Blair Jackson
John Dawson
Merl Saunders
Ian Anderson
Danny Sugarman
Carol Kaye
Matt Chook
Mary Valente
And the Goons

In memory of my cousin Cheri-Lynn Huss.

FOREWORD

Since the moment I bought my first guitar with money I won from a Los Angeles radio station at the age of ten, my interest in rock 'n' roll has never diminished. My first actual contact with rock-'n'-roll stardom came when I worked as a co-executive producer on a documentary video that featured the popular eighties group Air Supply.

When I started researching various groups in the hope of producing another documentary, I came across the story of Badfinger, a band that reached the rock world's highest plateau before succumbing to the dark side of the music business. Before long I was hooked. I spent days searching through microfilm for stories and obituaries on various dead artists. As I researched each artist or band, I found that their biographies contained many inaccuracies. My goal for this book was to put to rest any rumors or untrue stories regarding these artists. Through contacts I had made in the music business, I was able to interview many of the musicians, managers, and friends who were involved in the lives of the artists in this book.

I hope you find these stories as fascinating to read as it was for me to write them.

Gary J. Katz

CONTENTS

Contents

Duane Allman Slides 50 Feet in Fatal Motorcycle Accident

The Allman Brothers Band: (From left) Duane Allman, Berry Oakley, Gregg Allman, Butch Trucks, Jaimoe, and Dickey Betts. (Courtesy Berry Oakley)

ALLMAN BROTHERS BAND

Duane Allman

Berry Oakley

March 23, 1969, was the day of what they now call the Legendary Jacksonville Jam. After three hours of nonstop jamming, Duane Allman exclaimed, "Man, this is it." The Allman Brothers Band had been born. At first the band struggled, playing a grueling two-year schedule of five hundred one-nighters. Five roadies and six band members traveled in one van. The band eventually signed a contract with Capricorn Records and began recording their first album, *The Allman Brothers Band*. The reviews were excellent and their success soon reached national proportions. By the time the band recorded their second album, *Idlewild*, the Allman Brothers Band was already known as one of the finest in the rock and blues field.

Duane, a successful longtime sessions player, continued his studio work while the band's reputation began to grow. His guitar work with Eric Clapton on the Derek and the Dominoes' *Layla* album is considered some of his finest work.

During the recording of the band's fourth album in 1971, Allman took his first vacation in two years. While staying at the band's communal home, Big House, in Macon, Georgia, Duane paid a brief visit to Linda Oakley, the wife of bassist Berry Oakley, to wish her a happy birthday. On his way home, he swerved his motorcycle to avoid hitting a truck at an intersection. He lost control of the cycle and was pinned under it as it continued to travel another fifty feet. He was rushed to Macon Medical Center where he died on the operating table, on October 29, 1971—just one month before his twenty-fifth birthday. Hundreds of friends and family attended the funeral at Macon Memorial Chapel. Allman's guitar was placed in front of the casket while the band played "The Sky Is Crying."

A year and two weeks later, bassist Berry Oakley also died in a motorcycle accident on November 11, 1972, just three blocks from the site of Allman's fatal crash. Oakley was twenty-four years old.

Tragedy of Badfinger Two Members Commit Suicide

Badfinger. Pete Ham (far left), Tom Evans (far right). (Photo courtesy Apple Corp. Ltd)

BADFINGER

Pete Ham

Tom Evans

Originally known as the Iveys, Badfinger would become the first band signed to the Beatles' new Apple Corps Ltd label. With Paul McCartney writing their first big hit, "Come and Get It," the future looked bright for Badfinger band members Pete Ham, Tom Evans, Joey Molland, and Mike Gibbins. Between 1970 and 1974, Badfinger released four albums on the Apple label: *The Magic Christian*, *No Dice*, *Straight Up*, and *Ass*. Their biggest hit, "Day After Day," was produced by George Harrison and stayed on the charts for twelve weeks, climbing up to the No. 4 position in *Billboard* and to No. 1 in *Record World*. Other hits included "No Matter What" and "Baby Blue."

Enjoying a close relationship with the Beatles, Badfinger played on George Harrison's "All Things Must Past," John Lennon's "Imagine," and on Ringo Starr's "It Don't Come Easy." In 1971, Harrison took the band to New York to play at the Concert for Bangladesh. Pete Ham and Tom Evans also wrote the hit song "Without You," which Harry Nilsson and Mariah Carey took to the top of the charts. Badfinger did six American tours and became more popular in the United States than in Britain.

On one of their American tours in 1970, Badfinger met and signed a management agreement with New York businessman Stan Polley. Polley convinced the band to create an American corporation (Badfinger Enterprises Inc.) with Polley as president. He then took control of all financial dealings and put the band on a small weekly salary. In 1972, after negotiations for a new contract with Apple began to fall apart, Polley signed Badfinger to a six-record, $3-million contract with Warner Brothers. Warner paid $600,000 up front, but according to Joey Molland, the band never saw any of the money. Tension between the band members and management began to grow. Disagreements within the band became more frequent, and after completing their second Warner album, *Wish You Were Here*, Pete Ham left the group. Warner immediately started a lawsuit for breach of contract. Within two weeks, Ham was persuaded to rejoin the band.

With little money coming in and the Warner lawsuit still lingering over their heads, Pete Ham became depressed. For the first time in his life, his bank account was overdrawn. Stan Polley refused to send any money and did not return Pete's calls. Upon further investigation, Ham discovered that the money Stan Polley was holding for them had been spent by Polley on his lavish lifestyle. Due to the pending lawsuit, Warner soon pulled both Badfinger albums off the market and stopped all royalty payments to the band.

On the night of April 22, 1975, Pete Ham was at Tom Evans's house writing songs and discussing their money problems. Marianne Evans remembers that Ham was concerned about his girlfriend, Ann, who was pregnant and about to give birth to his first child. Ham and Tommy Evans drank and talked until about one A.M. Before leaving, Ham told Evans, "I know a way out." It was the last time Evans saw his longtime friend alive. On the morning of April 23, 1975, Ann found Ham hanging by a rope in the garage of his Surrey home. He was four days shy of his twenty-eighth birthday. The last line of his suicide note read, "Stan Polley is a soulless bastard." Two days later Polley called Ann to see if there was anything he could do for her. He also wanted her to make a statement saying that he had nothing to do with Pete Ham's death. Ann refused.

After a short breakup, Tom Evans and Joey Molland re-formed the group and recorded two more Badfinger albums, *Airwaves* and *Say No More*. An American concert promoter convinced the band to do another American tour. Only after the band arrived in America did they discover no tour dates were lined up. After literally starving in a rented house in the Midwest, the band returned to England, where Tom Evans was hit with a $5-million lawsuit by the same promoter. On the morning of November 18, 1983, Tom Evans's body was found hanging from a tree in his backyard. The cause of death, suicide by hanging. He was thirty-six years old.

Detroit

Original Supreme Florence Ballard Dies Penniless at 32

Florence Ballard. (Courtesy Motown Records)

FLORENCE BALLARD

After climbing up from poverty to the top of the charts with ten No. 1 songs in three years, Florence Ballard ended up back where she started, penniless and on welfare.

Ballard, Mary Wilson, and Diana Ross became the Supremes, one of the hottest female vocal groups of the 1960s and 1970s. Originally the Primettes, they were signed to Motown's Tamla label in 1960. They changed their name to the Supremes in 1961 and were without a hit until 1963 when they released "When the Lovelight Starts Shining Through His Eyes," which reached No. 23 on the pop charts. In 1964, when Holland-Dozier-Holland began to produce and write for the trio, the megahits began to flow. With Ross replacing Ballard as the lead singer, the next five singles all reached No. 1 on *Billboard*'s Top 40.

When an intense rivalry developed between Ballard and Ross, Ballard began drinking heavily. She became increasingly unreliable, and in 1967 she was forced out of the group. The downhill slide had begun. There was a short-lived marriage and an attempt at a solo career, which soon fizzled out; she lost her home through foreclosure and, with her three young daughters, moved into a two-family flat with her sister and mother.

During the early 1970s, Ballard sued Motown Records for $8 million, which she claimed was her share of record earnings. Ballard lost the case, and the spiral downward eventually led to a fatal heart attack. Ballard died in a Detroit hospital on February 22, 1976. She was thirty-two years old.

New York

Beatles' John Lennon Shot Dead in Front of Dakota Apartments

John Lennon.

THE BEATLES

Stu Sutcliff

John Lennon

The original lineup of the Beatles, formed in Liverpool in 1959, included John Lennon, guitar and vocals; Paul McCartney, guitar and vocals; George Harrison, guitar and vocals; Stuart Sutcliff, bass; and Pete Best on drums. After becoming a local success in Liverpool, the band began a grueling schedule of eight to ten hours each night in the clubs in Hamburg, Germany.

Stu Stucliff joined Lennon's band, Johnny and the Moondogs, after becoming friendly with Lennon in art school. Sutcliff was never more than a mediocre bass player, but Lennon was impressed with Sutcliff's flair for fashion and thought he gave the band the image Lennon was looking for. The band soon changed their name to the Silver Beatles as their popularity steadily grew.

Playing small clubs and town halls all across Liverpool sometimes led them to violent venues. Often while the band was playing the poorest and roughest sections of town, the local thugs, or teddy boys as they were called, would disrupt the show and start fights. One night Stu Sutcliff was thrown to the ground and savagely kicked in the head. If John Lennon hadn't pulled him out of the melee to safety, Sutcliff might have been killed.

During their stay in Hamburg, Sutcliff met a photographic assistant named Astrid Kirchner. They soon fell in love. It was

Astrid who talked Sutcliff into wearing his hair long and over his forehead. When the other members followed his lead, the Beatle haircut was born.

When it came out that George Harrison was under the age of eighteen, the age required by law to be in a club past curfew, the Beatles were soon on their way back home to Liverpool. A few months later Harrison turned eighteen and the band was once again off to Hamburg. Back together again, Sutcliff and Astrid were inseparable. It soon became apparent to the others that Sutcliff had no intention of leaving Astrid and would stay with her in Hamburg, and the Beatles returned home without him. It was during this time that Sutcliff started suffering from terrible headaches that would last for days on end.

Now under the management of Brian Epstein, the Beatles were scheduled to appear on April 13, 1962, at the Star Club in Hamburg. They looked forward to reuniting with Sutcliff. On the day of their departure they received a telegram from Astrid. Sutcliff had died in her arms on April 10, 1962, while being taken by ambulance to the hospital. An autopsy showed that he had died from a brain hemorrhage. He was twenty-two years old.

The early seventies were a turbulent time for John Lennon. Faced with deportation from the United States for a British drug charge, he and Yoko Ono, his second wife, separated for eighteen months. During this time Lennon stayed high on drugs and booze. Only when they reunited did his life start to fall into place. In 1975, the Lennons settled down to a quiet life in New York City. They were often seen walking through Central Park or shopping at the local stores.

Reversing their marriage roles, Lennon now took care of their son, Sean. He dropped out of the recording limelight for five years, resurfacing in 1980 with his new album *Double Fantasy*.

On the evening of December 8, 1980, Lennon and Yoko Ono went to the recording studio to work on his newest album, *Starting Over*. As they were leaving their apartment at the Dakota, a man approached and asked Lennon for his autograph. Captured by a photographer's camera, the man in the picture, Mark Chapman, became Lennon's assassin a few hours later. Upon returning from the studio at about eleven, Lennon stepped out of his limousine and was walking past the doorman's station under an archway when a voice called out, "Mr. Lennon." As Lennon turned to see who called him, shots rang out. Lennon shouted, "I'm shot," and staggered into the doorman's station. A nearby police car arrived and took him to the hospital, but he was dead when he arrived. Chapman made no attempt to flee and was taken into custody. Lennon was forty years old.

New York

Bloomfield Dies of Drug Overdose

Michael Bloomfield.

MICHAEL BLOOMFIELD

PAUL BUTTERFIELD

In his youth, Michael Bloomfield traveled to Chicago to learn the blues firsthand from legendary blues greats Muddy Waters, Howlin' Wolf, and Buddy Guy. Bloomfield soon earned a name for himself while playing with Nick Gravenites and the legendary harmonica player Charlie Musselwhite.

In 1965, Bloomfield joined the Butterfield Blues Band, playing lead guitar. The group, including guitarist Elvin Bishop, played the Newport Folk Festival and backed Bob Dylan in his first electric show that same year. Bloomfield also played on Dylan's "Like a Rolling Stone" and the LP *Highway 61 Revisited*.

After leaving Butterfield, Bloomfield formed the Electric Flag with singer Nick Gravenites, drummer Buddy Miles, Barry Goldberg on keyboards, and Harvey Brooks on bass and horns. They released the LP *A Long Time Coming* in 1968 and had finished their second album when Bloomfield decided to leave the group. He then recorded the now famous Super Sessions with Al Kooper and Stephen Stills.

Between 1969 and 1976, Bloomfield continued to record albums with various musicians. KGB on MCA would be his last attempt to form a supergroup. When this failed, Bloomfield worked on a series of movie sound tracks.

On February 15, 1981, Michael Bloomfield was found dead at the age of thirty-six, at his home in New York. The coroner's report stated that he died due to a drug overdose. According to Harvey Brooks, Bloomfield had a chemical imbalance that forced him to stay awake for days at a time. He maintained that Bloomfield took various drugs in a desperate attempt to fall asleep.

After the departure of Bloomfield from the Butterfield Blues Band in 1968, Paul Butterfield and Elvin Bishop continued to tour and record. Turning more in an R&B direction, Butterfield, Bishop, and Mark Naftalin added a horn section, which included David Sanborn and Charles Dinwiddie, with Phillip Wilson playing drums. In 1969, the group released the LP *Keep on Moving* with "Sometimes I Just Feel Like Smilin'," and a two-disc live album followed in 1971. *Golden Butter—Best Of* would be their last release before disbanding.

Butterfield formed the group Better Days and continued to record until 1976. He also appeared at the Band's Last Waltz party in 1976 and toured with both Levon Helm and Rick Danko. The 1981 LP *North-South* was the last album Butterfield recorded. On May 4, 1987, Butterfield was found dead at forty-four years of age in his apartment in Los Angeles. Years of drug and alcohol abuse had finally taken their toll and claimed another victim.

Miami

Tommy Bolin Found Dead in Miami Hotel

Tommy Bolin.

TOMMY BOLIN

Born in Sioux City, Iowa, in 1951, Bolin formed his first band, Zephyr, in Denver in 1968. He recorded two albums with the band, *Zephyr*, released in 1970, and *Going Back to Colorado* in 1971, before going on the road with blues legend Albert King. After a year on the road with King, Bolin worked on expanding his talent in the jazz-rock scene in New York City.

With the departure of Joe Walsh from the James Gang, the band recruited Canadian-based guitarist Dom Troiano and vocalist Roy Kenner. The albums *Straight Shooter* and *Passin' Thru*, both recorded in 1972, were regarded as poor attempts to regain the popularity that was lost when Walsh left the band. When Troiano left to join the Guess Who, Walsh suggested to his ex–band members that they recuit Tommy Bolin.

Joining the band in 1973, Bolin cowrote all but one song on the 1973 release *Bang*. But despite Bolin's creative skills, both *Bang* and their 1974 release, *Miami*, sold poorly. The band split up after Bolin was invited to join Deep Purple.

Replacing Richie Blackmore in mid-1975, Bolin helped cowrite the album *Come Taste the Band*. Just making the Top 20 in the United Kingdom, the album charted at only No. 43 in America. Soon after, their company started releasing compilations, and in the summer of 1976, the band broke up.

Now recording as a solo act, Bolin released his first solo album, *Teaser*, with Jan Hammer. His second solo release, *Private Eyes*, followed in 1976 and featured ex–Vanilla Fudge keyboard player Mark Stein. While the band was on the road touring and promoting *Private Eyes*, Bolin was found dead in his hotel room on December 4, 1976. The official report concluded that Bolin had died from an accidental drug overdose. He was twenty-five years old.

London

Led Zeppelin's Drummer, John Bonham, Found Dead After Vodka Binge

John Bonham. (Courtesy Herb Green)

JOHN BONHAM

Led Zeppelin was originally known as the New Yardbirds. Guitarist Jimmy Page recruited singer Robert Plant, bass and keyboard player John Paul Jones, and drummer John Bonham. Between 1969 and 1980, Led Zeppelin charted four Top 20 singles, one Top 30, and one Top 40. Their most famous recording, "Stairway to Heaven," on their *Led Zeppelin IV* album, was never released as a single. However, the album itself reached the top of the charts in both the United Kingdom and the United States, and their U.S. tours broke many existing box-office records.

Nicknamed Bonzo, John Bonham, born May 31, 1948, was a heavy drinker. Jethro Tull bass player Dave Pegg, a longtime friend and drinking partner, remembers, "I started playing in the band the Way of Life when Bonzo and I were just teenagers. When the parties started, they usually continued until after the sun came up the next morning. With only a few hours of sleep, Bonzo would be ready to start drinking all over again.

"There was this time in L.A. when Zeppelin was playing the Forum and I was playing at the Troubadour in the folk-rock group Fairport Convention. After Zeppelin's gig, they all came over to the Troubadour and the party began. In fact, Zeppelin got up onstage and jammed with us, which was a great thing to happen. Bonzo and I were drinking pitchers of beer one after another."

As it got closer to closing time, Peter Grant, Zeppelin's manager, was able to convince a nearby club owner to open his bar for the band. The party lasted until about seven A.M when police raided the club. Nearly passed out, Bonham and Pegg hid behind an amplifier. About two hours later they were able to leave undetected. Both men then returned to their hotel rooms.

At about eleven-thirty that morning, Bonham called Pegg to meet him for lunch at Barney's Beanery, a popular L.A. hangout. As soon as Pegg arrived, the drinking started. At three P.M, Pegg reminded Bonham that he had a four-thirty P.M. flight to Hawaii for a gig the next day. Bonham told Pegg not to worry about it, he would make the flight. At six-thirty P.M. they were still at Barney's drinking tequila.

Returning to Pegg's hotel, Bonham pushed Pegg fully clothed into the swimming pool. Bonham then took off all his clothes and jumped into the pool. Leaving Bonham at poolside, Pegg changed and left for his eight P.M. gig at the Troubadour. At about one A.M. Pegg received a phone call from Bonham, who was still at Pegg's hotel. "You're not going to believe this," Bonham said. He had just awakened at the side of the pool with all his clothes and money gone. He wasn't sure where he was except that he knew he was in L.A. and was supposed to be in Hawaii. "We ended up giving him some of our clothes and bought him a plane ticket. He was soon on his way to Hawaii."

On September 25, 1980, after a night of heavy drinking, John Bonham died of asphyxiation from his own vomit. It was estimated that he had drunk more than forty shots of vodka while spending the last hours of his life at the home of guitarist Jimmy Page. Led Zeppelin was in rehearsals for a worldwide tour at the time of his death. His funeral was held at Rushock parish church near his farm in Worcestershire. Close to three hundred fellow musicians and fans were at the service. John Bonham was thirty-two years old.

Sweden

Tour Bus Accident Kills Metallica Bass Player

Cliff Burton.

CLIFF BURTON

For Cliff Burton, Lars Ulrich, James Hetfield, and Kirk Hammett, Metallica's 1986 European tour started out a little different from any of their preceding tours. This time Metallica were the headliners rather than a supporting act.

The group arrived in Cardiff, Wales, on September 10. Guitar tech John Marshall played rhythm guitar for Hatfield, who was recovering from a broken arm. He played twelve shows before Hatfield resumed the stage in Stockholm, Sweden, on September 26. With the band now a hundred percent, they all felt a great deal of relief. The next two months of touring should be a breeze.

After the show, they boarded their tour bus for the long trip to their next show, in Copenhagen. Among the crew members traveling with them were drum tech Flemming Larson, guitar tech John Marshall, Aidan Mullen, and road manager Bobby Schneider. The driver was an Englishman who had been hired for the tour. At about six-thirty A.M., on September 27, 1986, driving down a two-way highway, the bus started to veer off to the right. Sharply turning the wheel to the left, the bus driver overcorrected and the rear end started to fishtail completely around. At the same time, the bus was bouncing up and down while rocking back and forth on its wheels. The crew and band members were literally bounced right out of their bunks. Loose objects inside the bus were flying everywhere. Once the bus slid into the soft dirt shoulder of the road, it turned over on its side and came to a rest.

Dazed and confused, Hammett was able to make his way to an emergency door and was soon outside the toppled bus. One by one the other band members staggered out. Ulrich suffered a broken toe, Hammett had a black eye, and Schneider had shattered two ribs. But these were all superficial wounds compared to what Hammett found when he made his way out of the bus.

Burton, who was sleeping in a upper bunk on the right rear side of the bus, was apparently thrown halfway through his window. As the bus came to rest on its side, Burton was pinned underneath the wreckage. When Hammett got to Burton, his body was limp and lifeless. Cliff Burton, the twenty-four-year-old bass player for Metallica, was dead. Two days later, Metallica, minus Cliff Burton, returned home to America.

Los Angeles

Ex-Byrd Gene Clark Dead at 46

The Byrds. Gene Clark (top right); Michael Clarke (center). (Courtesy Sony Music)

THE BYRDS

Gene Clark

Gram Parsons

Clarence White

Michael Clarke

Born Harold Eugene Clark in Tipton, Missouri, on November 19, 1944, Gene Clark got his start as a member of the folk group the New Christy Minstrels. In 1964, Clark cofounded the folk-rock group the Byrds with Rodger McGuinn, David Crosby, Chris Hillman, and Michael Clarke. The Byrds first single, "Mr. Tambourine Man," written by Bob Dylan, climbed to No. 1 on the national pop charts. Clark would enjoy two more Top 20 songs with the Byrds before departing in 1966, due to problems associated with touring.

Teaming up with bluegrass musician Doug Dillard, the duo would record two albums under the name Dillard and Clark. Clark then went on to record several solo albums.

In 1973, after a number of personnel changes, the Byrds' original members got together for a reunion. This was short-lived as the band was neither a commercial nor a critical success. In 1979, Clark, Hillman, and McGuinn teamed again and released the song "Don't You Write Her Off," which reached the Top 40. But Clark again wanted to concentrate on a solo career and soon left the group.

Teaming up with drummer Michael Clarke in 1984, Clark started touring in "Tribute to the Byrds." During this time, he was also able to break free from a drug and alcohol problem he had had throughout most of his career.

In January 1991, all five original members of the Byrds were reunited and inducted into the Rock 'n' Roll Hall of Fame. This would be the last time that all the members were together. Five months later, on May 24, 1991, Gene Clark was found dead in his San Fernando Valley home. He had apparently suffered a heart attack after undergoing considerable dental work that was causing him great pain, and for which he was taking a prescribed painkiller. However, the coroner's report stated that Clark had died from natural causes. He was forty-six years old.

Born on November 5, 1946, and growing up in Waycross, Georgia, Gram Parsons experienced loss at an early age. At thirteen, his father, singer-songwriter Coon Dog Connor, committed suicide, and his mother, an alcoholic, died on Gram's graduation day from high school.

Playing in various bands since 1963, Parsons was thrust into the limelight with *Sweetheart of the Rodeo*, recorded in 1968 when Parsons was a member of The Byrds. The following year, he formed the Flying Burrito Brothers with ex-Byrd Chris Hillman. Hanging around with the Rolling Stones, Parsons appeared on their album's *Sticky Fingers*, 1971, and *Exile on Main Street*, 1972. His solo album, *GP*, released in 1973, featured Emmylou Harris, Rich Grech, James Burton, and Glen D. Hardin. Parsons, an alcoholic, was estranged from his wife when his house mysteriously burned down. Working on his second LP with Harris, Parsons checked into a motel in Joshua Tree, California. It was there, on September 19, 1973, that Parsons died of heart failure.

Parsons made it clear to friends that upon his death, he

wished to be cremated. Family members, not honoring his wishes, took his body for burial. His manager, Phil Kaufman, with friend Michael Martin, stole the body and carried out Parsons's wishes, spreading his ashes at Cap Rock. Gram Parsons was twenty-six years old.

Clarence White, born June 6, 1944, joined the Byrds in the winter of 1968. On July 14, 1973, while loading equipment into a van after finishing a gig in California, White was struck and killed by a car driven by a drunk driver. Clarence White was twenty-nine years old.

On December 19, 1993, ex-Byrds drummer Michael Clarke died of liver failure at his Treasure Island, Florida, home. Michael Clarke was fifty years old.

Canned Heat Guitarist Alan Wilson Found Dead in Singer's Backyard

Canned Heat. Alan Wilson (second from left), and Bob Hite (third from left)

CANNED HEAT

Alan "Blind Owl" Wilson

Bob "The Bear" Hite

Formed in 1966 by Bob "The Bear" Hite and Alan "Blind Owl" Wilson, Canned Heat became one of the music world's top white blues bands with the release of their first LP and the exposure the band received at the Monterey Pop Festival in 1967. Shortly before recording their second LP, *Boogie*, drummer Bob Cook was replaced by Adolpho "Fito" de la Parra. This album produced two Top 20 hits for the band. "On the Road Again" would chart at No. 16 and "Going up the Country" at No. 11.

After the release of their 1969 LP, *Living the Blues*, *Hallelujah*, ex-Zappa band member Harry Vestine left the group and was replaced by Harry Mandel. The band would also perform at Woodstock that year.

Alan Wilson, a music-major graduate of Boston University, was considered by some to be a musical genius. According to Eugene Skuratoticz, the band's current manager, Wilson suffered from frequent bouts of depression. On the night of September 2, 1970, the night before the band was to start a European tour, Wilson climbed into his sleeping bag behind Bob Hite's house in Topanga Canyon. The next morning he was found dead. The official report recorded Wilson's death as a drug overdose, but many who knew him believe it was a suicide. According to Skuratoticz, Wilson was free of drugs at the time of his death. He was twenty-seven.

31

Although many thought the death of Wilson tore out the heart of the band, Canned Heat continued to perform and record. Between 1972 and 1974, the band released three more LPs. These met with only moderate success, and soon the band was dropped from their record label.

Depressed at being dropped, Hite began to sink deeper into drugs to ease the pain. On the night of April 6, 1981, Canned Heat was playing a local L.A. club, and after their set, Hite complained of not feeling well. He was taken home where he lay down on the living room sofa to rest for a while. Bob Hite never woke up. The official report stated that Hite had died from a drug-induced heart attack. He was thirty-six years old.

Today Fito de la Parra's band carries on the name Canned Heat. A new LP is planned as a tribute to both Wilson and Hite.

Los Angeles

Karen Carpenter Suffers Fatal Heart Attack, Dead at 32

The Carpenters. (Courtesy A&M Records)

KAREN CARPENTER

Karen Carpenter, together with her brother Richard, would become one of the world's biggest acts in the 1970s. With Richard on piano and Karen on drums, the two recruited bass player Wes Jacobs, and after winning a "battle of the bands" at the Hollywood Bowl in 1966 (originally from New Haven, Connecticut, the Carpenters had moved to Downey, California, in 1963), the trio won an RCA contract. However, the two albums recorded on the label were never released and the trio disbanded.

After a period of playing in the band Spectrum, the Carpenters were signed as a duo to A&M Records in 1969. A cover of the Beatles' "Ticket to Ride" landed them in the charts at No. 54. The title track of their second LP, "Close to You," written by Bert Bacharach, was the duo's first No. 1 single. From then on, the Carpenters reached the Top 40 twenty times, with twelve of the entries in the Top 10. They sold more than 30 million records and won the 1970 Best New Artist Grammy Award.

By 1974, Karen Carpenter's health was beginning to fail. The Carpenters canceled their 1975 European tour because of her nervous and physical exhaustion. She was bedridden for six weeks, and it was later determined that Karen Carpenter was suffering from anorexia nervosa.

The Carpenters' last album, *Made in America*, released in 1981, met with only moderate success. Carpenter's 1980 marriage to real-estate developer Paul Bloch collapsed shortly before she was found unconscious at her parents' home in Downey, California. Just one month shy of her thirty-third birthday, on February 4, 1983, Karen Carpenter was rushed to the hospital but never regained consciousness. The coroner concluded the cause of death to be cardiac arrest brought on by chemical imbalances associated with anorexia.

New York

Kiss Drummer Eric Carr Dies of Cancer in Manhattan Hospital

Eric Carr. (Courtesy Kayos Productions Inc.)

ERIC CARR

Originally formed in 1972, Kiss consisted of Gene Simmons, Paul Stanley, Ace Frehley, and Peter Criss. The band became famous for their wild, cartoonlike face makeup, a fire-breathing bass player, glittering costumes, and flash bombs. Marvel Comics paid them the ultimate tribute by publishing a Kiss comic book. Between 1974 and 1989, Kiss recorded twenty-one albums. Nine singles would reach the Top 40 in *Billboard's* pop charts.

By 1977, Kiss's popularity had reached the point where their memorabilia and products were instant sellouts. When the press released the news that a solo album by each band member would soon be available, all four albums went platinum before their release date.

Claiming he could no longer cope with face makeup, drummer Peter Criss quit in 1980. He was replaced by Brooklyn musician Eric Carr. Carr fit the bill well and recorded eight LPs with the group.

A series of personnel changes started when Frehley left the band. He was replaced by Vince Cusano, who then quit after finishing their world tour. Cusano was replaced by Mark St. John. Ex-Blackjack guitarist Bruce Kulick then replaced St. John after he developed a debilitating illness.

In 1983, after changing record labels, Kiss abandoned their face makeup and recorded their first naked-face LP, *Lick It Up*. This was followed by the 1984 LP *Animalize*, which reached the Top 10 in both the United States and the United Kingdom. Although their albums did well, Kiss did not produce another Top 40 single until the 1990 hit "Forever."

Hospitalized after suffering a cerebral hemorrhage in September of 1991, Eric Carr died of cancer on Sunday, November 24, 1991, at Bellevue Hospital in Manhattan. He was forty-one years old.

London

Mama Cass, Pop Singer, Star of the Mamas & the Papas, Dies of Fatal Heart Attack After Choking on a Ham Sandwich

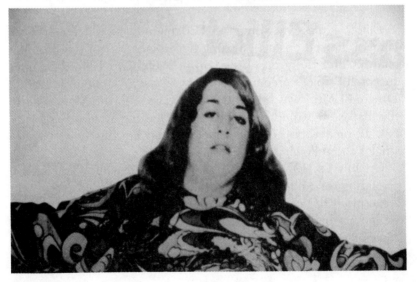

Mama Cass.

"MAMA" CASS ELLIOT

Born Ellen Naomi Cohen, on February 19, 1941, Cass Elliot was best known to her many fans as "Mama" Cass, a member of the legendary sixties vocal group the Mamas and the Papas. The quartet was formed in New York City in 1963 and consisted of John Phillips, Michelle Phillips, Denny Doherty, and Cass Elliot. Elliot and Doherty had played together in the Mugwumps with future Lovin' Spoonful guitarist Zal Yanovsky. Moving the group to Los Angeles in 1964, John Phillips was able to secure a recording contract on Lou Adler's newly formed label, Dunhill. With hits like "California Dreamin'" and "Monday, Monday," which gave the group their first No. 1 single, the Mamas and the Papas quickly became international rock stars.

Elliot, a massive woman at 250 pounds, would cheerfully laugh at herself onstage, making her weight part of the group's charm. After the group broke up in 1968, Cass Elliot began a successful solo career. Her first release, "Dream a Little Dream of Me," was billed as Mama Cass with the Mamas and the Papas. It would be her highest-charting single, reaching No. 12 on the pop charts. Elliot charted her last two Top 40 singles the following year.

On July 29, 1974, Mama Cass Elliot died while in London preparing for a concert. News that she had died by choking on a sandwich began to circulate quickly after her physician stated her probable cause of death. However, five days later the coroner reported that Cass Elliot had died of a heart attack, apparently induced by choking and her being overweight.

Singer Harry Chapin Killed on Long Island Expressway

Harry Chapin.

HARRY CHAPIN

Born December 7, 1942, the son of swing-era drummer Jim Chapin, Harry began appreciating music at an early age. As a child, Harry played the trumpet before switching to the guitar. His music career was interrupted while he studied at the Air Force Academy and Cornell University. Although still involved in music, Chapin set his sights on film and in 1969 was nominated for an Oscar for a silent documentary called *Legendary Champions*.

Playing on and off since 1964 with his father and brothers, Tom and Stephen, Harry helped write the songs for their 1970 LP, *Chapin Brothers*. By 1972, Harry was about to emerge as the star of the family with the release of his solo LP *Heads and Tales*. The LP included the hit song "Taxi," which would be Harry's first song to chart on *Billboard*'s Top 40, at No. 24.

Chapin soon followed up with the 1972 release *Sniper and Other Love Stories* and in 1973 with *Short Stories*. But it would be his 1974 release, *Verities and Balderdash*, that would yield him a No. 1 hit with the single "Cats in the Cradle." It would be another six years before Chapin charted again with the release of "Sequel" in 1980.

On July 16, 1981, Chapin was driving his 1975 Volkswagen on the Long Island Expressway when he apparently had car problems. Putting on his emergency blinkers, Chapin tried to change lanes so he could exit the expressway. He was hit from behind by a tractor-trailer traveling about 55 mph. The impact crushed the rear end of Chapin's car, creating sparks that ignited the fuel tank. Although he was pulled from the wreckage before he was badly burned, Chapin died, apparently from the force of the crash. He was thirty-eight years old.

San Francisco

Quicksilver's Cipollina Dead at 45

John Cipollina.

JOHN CIPOLLINA

Quicksilver Messenger Service was formed in 1965, but it was three years before they signed a recording contract with Capitol Records.

The original lineup consisted of John Cipollina, Gary Duncan, Greg Elmore, David Freiberg, and Jim Murray. Murray left in 1966 to study the sitar. His replacement, New York musician Dino Valenti, was jailed on drug charges and didn't join the band until 1970.

Quicksilver's self-titled debut album, released in the summer of 1968, was made up mostly of their stage act. The lead cut, "Pride of Man," would get considerable radio play. The album, however, received mixed reviews and sold only modestly. As a showcase for the band, the album allowed each member to strut his stuff.

Happy Trails, their second album, was recorded live at the Filmores West and East. It is considered by many to be their finest recorded work. Its first side consisted solely of a twenty-five-minute jam on Bo Diddley's "Who Do You Love," followed by a seven-minute version of Diddley's "Mona" on side two.

Following the success of *Happy Trails*, Gary Duncan shocked the band by deciding to leave on the last day of 1968. Keyboard ace Nicky Hopkins was recruited and filled in on keyboards for Duncan's guitar.

The band, now consisting of Cipollina, Freiberg, Elmore, and Hopkins, recorded the album *Shady Grove* in 1969. *Shady Grove* ushered in Quicksilver's new sound, mainly due to Hopkins. The album sold about as well as its predecessor in spite of the band's never touring behind it.

Gary Duncan was asked to sit in with the band on a New

Year's Eve show in 1969–70, exactly one year after he left. He also brought in Dino Valenti, whom he'd been playing with during the year. Quicksilver was now a sextet. Their 1970 release, *Just for Love*, would provide the group with their highest-charting single, "Fresh Air," written by Valenti. The follow-up album, *What About Me*, released in 1971, also did well, but marked the end of the original Quicksilver Messenger Service. At the end of 1970, prior to the album's release, John Cipollina left the group to form a new band called Copperhead.

With Copperhead breaking up soon after its formation, Cipollina played in a dozen bands between 1970 and the summer of 1975, when a Quicksilver reunion took place. They recorded the reunion album *Solid Silver*, but by most accounts, the album was disappointing. In 1977, the band finally parted.

On May 29, 1989, John Cipollina died of liver failure at the age of forty-five. In his honor, Freiberg, Duncan, Elmore, and Hopkins played a tribute concert in San Francisco at the reopened Filmore.

Seattle

Kurt Cobain Commits Suicide

Nirvana. Krist Noveselic (left), Kurt Cobain (center), David Grohl (right). (Courtesy Geffen Records)

KURT COBAIN

Born in Aberdeen, Washington, a logging town about one hundred miles southwest of Seattle, in 1967, Kurt Cobain, together with bassist Krist Novoselic, formed the grunge-rock group Nirvana in 1986. Playing with various drummers during this time, the band was signed to a small local label and released their first album, called *Bleach*. With the addition of drummer Dave Grohl, the band soon signed a new record deal with Geffen Records in 1991. By 1992, Nirvana was on their way to the top, being nominated at the MTV Music Awards for best new artist and best alternative-music video. Record sales for their album *Nevermind* would exceed 5 million copies in the United States alone.

Cobain was troubled as a youth, and his lyrics defined the alienated attitudes of his generation. He was addicted to heroin, and his life became a series of roller-coaster rides that took him deep within the abyss of his distraught mind.

Many believed his marriage to rock singer Courtney Love and the 1992 birth of his daughter, Frances Bean, would be his salvation. His love for his baby girl was apparent, but it was not enough to keep him straight. He and Courtney were known for their heavy drug use. The couple soon found themselves in a custody battle to keep their nineteen-month-old daughter. Rumors started circulating that their marriage was falling apart and that the band would soon break up. They had recently dropped out as the headliners for the Lollapalooza '94 tour. Their management stated the reason to be "health problems within the band."

One month before his death, while on tour in Rome, an apparent suicide attempt placed Cobain in a coma. His management released a statement saying that his drug and alcohol overdose was an accident. Soon after returning to Seattle,

Cobain locked himself in a room with a gun. The police report stated that four revolvers, twenty-five boxes of ammunition, and an assortment of pills were taken from the home. Cobain was committed to a drug-rehab center in L.A. by Love, but walked out after spending just forty-eight hours at the center.

Six days after Cobain was reported missing from the rehab center, his body was found on April 8, 1994, by an electrician who came to install an alarm system in a room over the garage of his house. Cobain was lying on his back, dressed in jeans, shirt, and sneakers, with a shotgun on top of him. He had shot himself once through the left temple. A suicide note was found next to his body, along with some other personal items.

In an interview with KNBC-TV news, the electrician stated that Cobain's suicide note was covered in dirt from a potted plant and ended with the words "I love you, I love you." Kurt Cobain was twenty-seven years old.

Chippenham

Rock-'n'-Roll Great Eddie Cochran Dies in Car Crash Near Wiltshire

Eddie Cochran.

EDDIE COCHRAN

Born Edward Ray Cochrane in Oklahoma City, Oklahoma, on October 3, 1938, Cochran would become one of the top white rock-'n'-roll stars of the 1950s.

After moving to Bell Gardens, California, in 1953, Cochran first worked with Hank Cochran (no relation) as the Cochran Brothers. When Hank left to pursue a career in country music, Eddie signed with Liberty Records. Known as a dynamite live performer, Cochran soon proved he was a much better guitar player and singer than most of his contemporaries, and by 1957 the hits began.

"Sittin' in the Balcony" was Cochran's first song to break into *Billboard's* Top 20. The rock-'n'-roll classic "Summertime Blues" propelled Cochran into the Top 10. Cochran also appeared in three motion pictures, *The Girl Can't Help It*, *Untamed Youth*, and *Go, Johnny, Go!*

In 1959, Cochran recorded a version of "Three Stars," dedicated to the memories of Buddy Holly, Richie Valens, and the Big Bopper, who were killed in a plane crash that year. He was soon to suffer a similar fate. Following a triumphant U.K. tour with Gene Vincent, Cochran was killed in a car crash in Chippenham, Wiltshire, England on April 17, 1960. Gene Vincent was injured in the crash.

Eddie Cochran was inducted into the Rock 'n' Roll Hall of Fame in 1987.

Drug Overdose Kills Association Bass Player Brian Cole

The Association. (Courtesy Photofest)

BRIAN COLE

As the bass player in the soft-rock group the Association, Brian Cole would enjoy seven songs in the Top 40 between 1966 and 1968. Two of these songs would top the charts at No. 1.

Formed in 1965 by Russ Giguere, Terry Kirkman, Gary Alexander, Jim Yester, Ted Bluechel, and Brian Cole, the group was best known for its vocal harmony. The entire group, all multi-instrumentalists, shared vocals as well. With their first release, "Along Comes Mary," reaching No. 7 in 1966, the group was on its way to fame and fortune despite allegations that the song was about marijuana.

Their second release, "Cherish," would bring them their first No. 1 single as well as three Grammys. Warner Brothers took over as the band's label and rereleased two of the group's earlier albums, *And Then ... Along Came Association* and *Renaissance*.

"Windy," the band's fourth release, was their second No. 1 hit single, followed by "Never My Love" resting in the No. 2 spot. They also opened the Monterey Pop Festival in the summer of 1967. The band would chart two more songs in the Top 40 before disbanding shorty thereafter. On August 2, 1973, Brian Cole was found dead of an accidental heroin overdose.

Los Angeles

Sam Cooke Slain in Los Angeles Motel

Sam Cooke. (Courtesy RCA Records)

SAM COOKE

Born on January 22, 1935, the son of a Chicago preacher, Sam Cooke applied his gospel training to pop music and soon began scoring such hits as "You Sent Me," "Another Saturday Night," and "Cupid." Unlike many music stars of the time, Cooke would often show up at the studio in a white shirt and tie, looking more like a businessman than a music star.

By the early 1960s, Sam Cooke was living the good life in a large Hollywood home with his wife and two children. In October 1964, Cooke had completed a screen test, and his career seemed ready for a major breakthrough into the movies. Dining out with some friends the night of December 10, 1964, Cooke picked up the beautiful model Elisa Boyer. Together they drove off to a small motel called the Hacienda. Boyer later told the police that Cooke dragged her into the motel room and started to rape her. When Cooke went into the bathroom for a moment, Boyer grabbed Cooke's pants and ran out the door to call police. Wearing only a topcoat, Cooke ran after her. When he couldn't find her, Cooke then went to see Bertha Lee Franklin, the motel manager, and began accusing her of hiding Boyer. Franklin wouldn't let him in; Cooke got into his car and started the motor. But instead of leaving, he decided to go back to Franklin's room; he kicked the door down. Franklin later told police that Cooke started beating her. When she was able to get free, Franklin ran and grabbed her pistol and fired three shots into the twenty-nine-year-old singer. Apparently the shots only wounded him. When Cooke came at her again, she clubbed him to death with a sticklike weapon. Police ruled the death a justifiable homicide.

Pop Singer Jim Croce and Five Others Perish in Plane Crash

Jim Croce.

JIM CROCE

Jim Croce, born January 10, 1943, grew up on the outskirts of Philadelphia, in a middle-class Italian family. While in college, he played in a number of bands and began writing songs. His love of music was so strong that after graduation he taught music to children in a Philadelphia high school.

In 1968, Croce and his first wife, Ingrid, moved to New York City where together they played the various coffeehouses in and around the Village. Never feeling at home in New York, they soon moved to Los Angeles where they met up with Croce's longtime friend Tommy West. Together with his musical partner Terry Cashman, West was able to convince Capitol Records to cut an album. But the lack of record sales forced Croce and his wife to return to the East Coast where he took a job driving a truck.

In 1970, West and Cashman convinced Croce to return to the music business. Together with guitarist Maury Muehleisen, he produced a tape that West sold to Phillips Records in England. Only after his death did his first album, *You Don't Mess Around With Jim*, make it to the No. 1 spot on the *Billboard* charts.

On September 20, 1973, after finishing a concert at Louisiana University, Croce and five others (including Maury Muehleisen) were killed when their plane struck a tree on takeoff from Natchitoches Municipal Airport. Croce's second album, *I Got a Name*, was finished just one week before his death and soon after took *Billboard*'s No. 2 spot.

Los Angeles

Bobby Darin Dies on Operating Table

Bobby Darin. (Courtesy Atlantic Records)

BOBBY DARIN

Born Robert Cassotto, on May 14, 1936, Bobby Darin fought his way from the streets of the Bronx to the streets of Beverly Hills. His father, Severio, was a small-time gangster who died before Darin was born. His mother, Vivian, gave up vaudeville when she married and ended up on welfare when her husband died.

Graduating from high school in 1953, Darin enrolled in college but dropped out after his first semester. A talented musician who could play piano, guitar, and the drums, he spent his summers in the Catskills playing in bands or working as master of ceremonies, and on some occasions, as a busboy. In 1957, Darin was signed to Atco Records, and the following year his career took off with his recording of "Splish Splash." Over one hundred thousand copies were sold in just three weeks. For his recording of "Mack the Knife," Darin received two Grammys: Best New Performer of 1959 and Best Single Record. Over the next several years Darin was prominent on the stages of Las Vegas, at New York's Copacabana, on TV, and in movies.

In 1960, Darin married Sandra Dee and they had a son, Dodd Mitchell Cassotto. But by 1966, after trying a reconciliation, they were divorced. By the late 1960s, Darin started to speak out about his beliefs regarding the war in Vietnam. It was during this period that he was booed off the stage in Las Vegas for singing freedom songs and protest ballads. In 1973, he married Andrea Joy Yeager, a marriage that lasted only a few months. With his marriage behind him and the war in Vietnam over, Bobby soon made his comeback with a series of Las Vegas appearances.

As a child, Darin had suffered from rheumatic fever, which had damaged his heart. In 1971, two artificial valves were implanted in his heart. By December 1973, these valves were malfunctioning, and during a six-hour struggle, on December 20, 1973, four surgeons fought to save his life. "He was just too weak to recover," one of the doctors would later say. Bobby Darin's body was given to the UCLA Medical Research Department, per his wishes.

New York

Jazz Legend Dies at 65

Miles Davis. (Courtesy Starworld)

MILES DAVIS

Born in Alton, Illinois, on May 25, 1926, Miles Davis would become one of the most influential and popular jazz musicians of all time. He would also be considered one of the most controversial, willing to blaze new trails and change direction.

Studying music at New York's Juilliard School of Music, where he was considered a musical prodigy, Davis was soon playing trumpet alongside tenor-sax giant Charlie Parker. While playing with Parker, Davis helped to create the revolutionary new jazz style bebop.

Over the next twenty years, Davis recorded dozens of albums with such notable jazzmen as John Coltrane, Rex Garland, Philly Joe Jones, and Paul Chambers. Inspired by the rock music of the 1960s, Davis put together a quintet that included pianist Herbie Hancock and drummer Tony Williams. Later groups included Chick Corea and John McLaughlin. His influence in rock music helped create the fusion between rock and jazz.

Losing most of his voice due to surgery on his vocal cords, Davis retired in 1976. He was physically drained and was suffering tremendous pain in his legs due to a car accident that had crushed them. He resented critics, who, he felt, didn't understand his creative direction, and the media for persistently focusing on his personal life. But, once rested, he was back and continued to record and perform until his death. Plagued with illness in his later years, Miles Davis died on September 28, 1991. He was suffering from pneumonia, which led to a stroke resulting in respiratory failure. He was sixty-five.

Brain Hemorrhage Kills Sandy Denny

Sandy Denny.

FAIRPORT CONVENTION

Martin Lamble

Sandy Denny

Formed in London in 1967, Fairport Convention consisted of Simon Nichol, Richard Thompson, Ashley Hutchings, and Shaun Frater. After just one gig, drummer Shaun Frater left the group and was replaced by Martin Lamble. Judy Dyble was the group's first female singer, joining about six months later. Ian Matthews soon joined, and the group recorded their first LP, entitled *Fairport Convention*.

In 1968, Sandy Denny replaced Dyble and the group soon recorded their second LP, *What We Did on Our Holiday*. Fiddle player Dave Swarbrick soon joined, replacing Matthews, and in 1969 the group released two LPs, *Unhalfbricking* and what would be considered their finest LP, *Liege & Lief*. According to bass player Dave Pegg, who joined Fairport in 1969, "Sandy Denny came from a folk-music background, while Fairport was more into the blues scene. Her influence can really be heard, and I think that had a lot to do with the tremendous success of the album." *Liege & Lief* would be hailed as Britain's first folk-rock album.

On May 12, 1969, Fairport was returning to London from a gig in Birmingham when the band's van slid out of control and crashed. Drummer Martin Lamble was killed in the crash along with a girlfriend of Richard Thompson's. Lamble was twenty years old.

As the band started to write and play more traditional folk

music, Sandy Denny decided to leave and pursue a solo career. Pegg recalls that "it was all quite strange because the guys that were playing rock wanted to be folkies, and the folkies decided they wanted to do their own thing." Soon after the departure of Denny, Ashley Hutchings left to start the folk-rock band Steeleye Spam. It was shortly after Hutchings's departure that Dave Pegg joined the band along with drummer Dave Mattacks.

The band carried on without replacing Denny. Between 1970 and 1974, the Fairport Convention went through many personnel changes, one of which was the departure of Richard Thompson in 1971. Pegg recalls, "We thought it was going to be a devastating blow when Richard left the band. He was our main writer, lead guitar player, and a fine singer. But somehow we managed to carry on." Simon Nichol also left the band shortly thereafter. Still, the band was able to release two more LPs.

In 1972, Pegg and Swarbrick, the two remaining members, were able to convince Trevor Lucas, who was Sandy Denny's fiancé, to produce an album as well as join the band. They persuaded Dave Mattacks to rejoin as well as Jerry Donohue, who had also played with the band. The result of this lineup was the album *Fairport Nine*. The band was soon touring again, and during this time Denny and Lucas were married.

With her husband now a member of Fairport, Denny sat in with the band on various occasions and, by 1974, was once again a member. Their first release was a live-album record at the Sydney Opera House called *Live Convention*.

With tension rife among band members, Mattacks once again decided to leave the band. Denny also left in the middle of recording their next LP, *Rising for the Moon*, in 1976. The band then disbanded for a time and regrouped in 1977. Denny continued her solo career, with her husband producing her albums. They bought a cottage in the country and she soon gave birth to a baby girl named Georgia.

The music scene in London was turning punk, while in Sydney it was just taking off. Lucas, a native of Australia, was in demand there as a producer. It was agreed that he would return to Sydney to advance his career. After he boarded his flight in mid-April 1978, Denny went to stay at a friend's house in London. The next day, Denny lost her balance and fell down a full flight of stairs. She was taken to the hospital in a coma. Lucas returned home the next day and was at her side when Denny died of a brain hemorrhage on April 21, 1978. She was thirty-seven years old.

Scottsdale, Arizona

Creedence Clearwater Revival Cofounder Dead at 48

Tom Fogerty (second from left).

TOM FOGERTY

As cofounder with his brother John of the highly successful sixties rock band Creedence Clearwater Revival, Tom Fogerty was part of the elite group of artists who obtained platinum-record status. In fact, the group received five platinum and five gold record awards for singles released between 1968 and 1971.

Originally called Tommy Fogerty & the Blue Velvets, the band was formed while the members attended high school in El Cerrito, California. Consisting of Tom and John Fogerty, Stu Cook, and Doug Clifford, the band first recorded as the Blue Velvets in 1959 for Orchestra Records. By 1964, they had signed with Fantasy and were recording under the name the Golliwogs. With their final name change to Creedence Clearwater Revival, the band finally reached the charts with the release of "Suzie Q" in 1968. The foursome would end up selling more than 86 million records, with eight Top 10 singles and six gold albums, before disbanding in October 1972.

Wanting to spend more time with his wife and children, Tom Fogerty left the group in 1971. He worked on some solo projects, but for the most part was not heard from. On September 6, 1990, Tom Fogerty died from respiratory failure stemming from tuberculosis. He was forty-eight years old.

Hollywood

Mysterious Death of Rock Star Suicide or Murder?

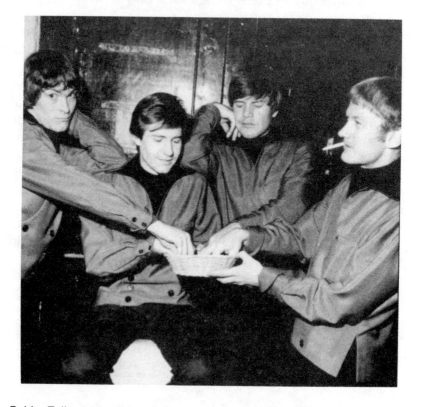

Bobby Fuller (second from left). (Courtesy Rhino Records)

BOBBY FULLER

Bobby Fuller began his career in El Paso, Texas, with his brother Randy, DeWayne Quirico, and Jim Reese. Known as the Bobby Fuller Four, the band played local dates for three years before packing up and moving to Los Angeles in 1964. Mustang Records, located at the time over a bank in a Hollywood building, had two of the first three eight-track recording machines in Los Angeles. Impressed by Mustang's state-of-the-art recording studio, Fuller soon signed with the label.

But success for Bobby Fuller was slow in coming, and by 1966 he became disenchanted with his career. Playing lots of small clubs started to take its toll. Fuller wanted to stop touring and concentrate on writing and recording. Only after "I Fought the Law" became a hit and soared to the top of the charts did Fuller start to realize his dream. Mustang, now needing more material to record, allowed Fuller to call his musical shots.

Fuller's success would not last long. On July 18, 1966, he was found dead in the front seat of his mother's car, which was parked in front of their Hollywood apartment. The official report labeled his death a suicide, a result of swallowing a large amount of gasoline. And yet a number of things simply 'idn't add up to a suicide. He had a hit song and had been ·n almost total musical freedom. On the day of his death he ⸝anning on buying a new Corvette. The fact that he was ·ʋ was never made public. His mother's car was never fingerprints. These and other facts surrounding his ·any believe that Bobby Fuller's death was a mur- ·ᵖ A police cover-up? A suicide? We are never 'he circumstances of Bobby Fuller's last

t Forest Lawn Cemetery in Burbank, ·ᵧ-two years old.

London

Heart Attack Claims Life of Pop Star Billy Fury

Billy Fury. (Courtesy Photofest)

BILLY FURY

Born in Liverpool on April 17, 1941, Fury would become one of Britain's biggest solo acts during the early sixties. After his first hit, "Maybe Tomorrow," released in 1959, Fury gained a reputation as the greatest, sexiest British rocker on the scene. He also starred in *I've Gotta Horse*, a film in which he played the role of a racehorse-loving pop star. Although Fury had a string of hits in the United Kingdom, he was never able to break into the Top 40 charts in the United States. He was best known in the United Kingdom for his hit songs "Halfway to Paradise," "Jealousy," "I'd Never Find Another You," "Like I've Never Been Gone," "When Will You Say I Love You," and "In Summer."

Fury suffered from rheumatic fever as a child and later developed heart problems; he underwent heart surgery in 1967 and semiretired to a farm in Sussex. During this period he played only a few dates and starred in the film *That'll Be the Day*, as rock idol Rocky Tempest. More surgery followed in 1975, and Fury once again retired until late 1982, when he attempted a comeback. He worked on the TV show *Unforgettable*, recorded an LP for Polydor, and planned a new tour. Shortly after finishing a recording session for a new album, Fury collapsed and died from a heart attack, on January 28, 1983. He was forty-one years old.

Los Angeles

Marvin Gaye Is Shot Dead by Father, Rev. Marvin Gaye, Sr., 70, Faces Charges in Son's Murder

Marvin Gaye. (Courtesy Motown Records)

MARVIN GAYE

TAMMI TERRELL

Born Marvin Pentz Gaye, Jr., on April 2, 1939 in Washington, D.C., Gaye sang as a child in his father's apostolic church. At fifteen, Gaye started singing doo-wop in the group the Rainbows and won a talent contest singing Harvey Fuqua's "The Ten Commandments of Love" (Fuqua was the judge). Following his father's wishes, Gaye joined the United States Air Force, but was released from duty for psychological reasons.

Soon after his release from the military, Gaye rejoined the Rainbows, now called the Marquees, but soon left to join Fuqua, whose group the Moonglows were recording for Chess Records. When the group went to Detroit, both Fuqua and Gaye signed with Tamla/Motown.

As a solo act, Gaye made the charts with the release of "Hitch Hike" in 1963. Altogether, Gaye would have a total of forty songs in *Billboard*'s Top 40. Eighteen made it to the Top 10, and three to No. 1. While at Motown, Gaye met and married Barry Gordy's sister, Ann. The marriage lasted from 1961 to 1975.

During the latter years of the sixties, Gaye recorded another seven Top 40 hits with Tammi Terrell. But their association was cut short when Terrell died of a brain tumor on March 16, 1970. Devastated by Terrell's death, Gaye stayed in seclusion for several months. Problems with drugs and the IRS led to his moving to Europe for three years. A second marriage, in 1977, came to a abrupt end when his wife left him for musician Teddy Pendergrass,

After many nominations, Gaye won a long overdue Grammy for Best R&B Performance in 1982. Two years later, on April 1, 1984, he was shot to death by his father following a quarrel at his father's house in Los Angeles. Marvin Gaye was inducted into the Rock 'n' Roll Hall of Fame in 1987.

Arlington

Drug-Induced Heart Attack Kills Little Feat Founder

Lowell George. (Courtesy Warner Brothers)

LOWELL GEORGE

Born in Arlington, Virginia, on April 13, 1945, Lowell George formed the blues/rock band Little Feat in 1969, having played earlier with Frank Zappa and the Mothers of Invention. It was Zappa who suggested that George start his own band and who helped pick the name Little Feat, based on George's tiny shoe size. Little Feat released their first album in 1971, with a group including ex-Zappa bassist Roy Estrada, Richie Hayward, and Bill Payne. Although the production was low-budget, the album was an impressive debut.

After the release of their second album, *Sailin' Shoes*, in 1972, Estrada left to join Captain Beefheart's Magic Band. George then recruited Kenny Gradney on bass, Sam Clayton on congas, and a second guitar player, Paul Barrere. The reception of their 1973 release, *Dixie Chicken*, was unenthusiastic, and the band soon split up for six months. They reformed and released another five albums before breaking up in 1979.

Now a solo act, George, together with Little Feat drummer Richie Hayward, embarked on a U.S. tour promoting his first solo LP, *Thanks, I'll Eat It Here*. On June 29, 1979, the day after a sellout concert in Washington, Lowell George suffered a fatal heart attack in his motel room in Arlington, Virginia. The coroner's report stated that his heart attack was induced by years of drug abuse. Lowell George was thirty-four years old.

Pop Music Sensation of the 1970s, Andy Gibb, Mysteriously Dies at Age 30 in Great Britain

Andy Gibb. (Courtesy RSO Records)

ANDY GIBB

Andrew Roy Gibb was born in Manchester, England, on March 5, 1958. Gibb would soon follow in the footsteps of his older brothers, Barry, Robin, and Maurice. Although many in the industry thought that Andy Gibb would become the fourth Bee Gee, he quickly became a pop music sensation of his own. He had his first No. 1 hit and became a pop teen idol by the age of nineteen. Between May 1977 and April 1978, he charted three No. 1 songs in a row. And by 1981, he would have a total of nine hit songs in the Top 40, resulting in four gold records and one platinum record.

In the early eighties Gibb cohosted the syndicated TV show *Solid Gold* and appeared in various stage productions. His romantic involvement with actress Victoria Principal was a staple in the news tabloids.

After his breakup with Principal, Gibb turned to drugs to ease the pain and was admitted to the Betty Ford Clinic for treatment of cocaine abuse. In 1987, he filed for bankruptcy in Miami, declaring less than $50,000 in assets and more then $1 million in debt.

By January 1988, a strong comeback seemed close at hand. Gibb's bankruptcy had been discharged; the singer had signed a new record deal with Island Records and was scheduled to start recording in the spring. According to a spokeswoman for Island Records, "Gibb was admitted to the John Radcliffe Hospital in Oxford on Monday for observation after complaining of stomach pains." He died the following Thursday, March 10, 1988, from an inflammatory heart virus. He was thirty years old.

London

Jethro Tull's Bassist, John Glascock, Dead at 28

Jethro Tull. (From the left) John Glascock, Ian Anderson, and
Barriemore Barlow. (Courtesy Chrysalis Records)

JOHN GLASCOCK

Tragedy shows its face in many ways. For John Glascock, it could have been avoided by a routine visit to the dentist. Glascock's first love was music, and mastering the bass guitar, he played in such bands as Chicken Shack, the Gods, Carmen, and finally the supergroup Jethro Tull.

While on a thirteen-week American tour with Carmen, Glascock met Barriemore Barlow, drummer for Jethro Tull. This was the start of a close and lasting friendship. When Carmen's record label announced that they were not renewing Carmen's contract, Barlow suggested to Ian Anderson that Glascock would make a good replacement for their departing bass player, Jeffrey Hammond. In December 1975, Glascock joined Jethro Tull and work began on the album *Too Old to Rock & Roll*.

Toward the end of a European tour, Glascock complained to Barlow of chest pains; Barlow told him not to worry, most likely it was just heartburn. But upon returning home to England, Glascock fell ill. Barlow suggested he see a doctor immediately.

The examination revealed that Glascock had a faulty heart valve. Knowing that his father had suffered from a similar ailment, Glascock thought his heart problem was hereditary. But further testing revealed that poison from a tooth abscess Glascock had neglected for over a year had actually poisoned his body, damaging the heart valve. Open-heart surgery and replacement of the valve was his only option.

Once recovered, Glascock resumed rehearsals. But his circulation was not what it had been before the surgery, and he complained that his fingers would go numb from time to time. A short time later Glascock decided to leave the band and was replaced by Dave Pegg.

While on tour in Los Angeles, Barlow decided that he'd had enough of touring with Jethro Tull. He called Glascock to see if he would be interested in starting a new band. Barlow recalls that John was ecstatic and couldn't wait to start. Barlow then contacted David Allen, who was the main singer and songwriter for Carmen. Allen agreed to join the two and booked a flight for London that afternoon so he and Glascock could start rehearsals. Barlow planned to meet them in London once the Jethro Tull tour was over. The next day, on November 21, 1979, Barlow received a call from John's girlfriend; Glascock had passed away that morning. Barlow later learned that Glascock's doctor had been trying to get John to go back into the hospital; his body had rejected the new heart valve.

Although John Glascock had spent nearly four years with Jethro Tull and had completed two European and four American tours, he was virtually broke at the time of his death. Barriemore Barlow and another friend, Tommy Vance, paid for his funeral. John Glascock was twenty-eight years old.

San Francisco

Grateful Dead's Singer, Songwriter Ron "Pigpen" McKernan Dead at 27

Ron "Pigpen" McKernan. (Courtesy Herb Green)

GRATEFUL DEAD

Ron "Pigpen" McKernan

Keith Godchaux

Brent Mydland

As one of the original members of the Grateful Dead, Ron "Pigpen" McKernan was known for his exceptional blues singing and blues harp. In the early 1960s, the Grateful Dead, playing their psychedelic acid rock, grew quickly into a great improvisational rock band. But the Dead lifestyle proved to be deadly for Ron McKernan.

Born in the small working-class community of San Bruno, just south of San Francisco, on September 8, 1945, McKernan grew up listening to everything from Lightnin' Hopkins to Big Joe Turner to the Coasters. Ron's father, Phil, was a radio personality in Berkeley and had built up a large record collection. This was the musical inheritance that influenced Ron.

In the early fifties, the McKernans moved to East Palo Alto, which at the time was a working-class neighborhood of both black and white families. Due to his early blues influence, Ron was naturally drawn to black people and black music. During his high school years, he would spend his free time listening to and learning blues piano, guitar, and harmonica.

By age fourteen, McKernan had met Jerry Garcia and they started hanging out together and were soon well accepted in the black blues scene. According to Garcia, "the blacks loved

Pigpen. They loved that he played the blues and was a genuine person. He wasn't a white person trying to be black."

In a 1970 interview, McKernan stated, "I was hanging around the Chateau in Palo Alto around 1962, give or take a century, and we started to drink some wine once in a while—Ripple wine. Then we graduated to Hombre and Thunderbird." Before long McKernan was seldom without a bottle of cheap wine. During this time he and Garcia formed the Zodiacs.

By 1964, Mother McCree's Uptown Jug Champions were formed, evolving soon after into the Warlocks and, by early 1967, into the Greatful Dead. The band moved to San Francisco.

The group signed with Warner Bros. in 1967. *Workingman's Dead* and *American Beauty*, both released in 1970, showcased the band's writing skill with their blues, country, and folk-styled originals. During 1970, McKernan's health began to deteriorate, and by 1971 the ravages of many years of alcohol abuse began to show. Diagnosed with advanced liver disease, he was told to stop drinking. By August of 1971, McKernan was so frail that he could no longer tour with the band and was hospitalized. By the end of September, the band hired Keith Godchaux to replace him. Godchaux continued to play with the band even after McKernan returned to limited performing in early December.

Although Pigpen did not drink for the last seventeen months of his life, his liver disease continued to progress. On the night of March 8, 1973, he was found by his landlord lying on the floor next to his bed. He had apparently been dead for two days. The official autopsy concluded that the cause of death was a "massive gastrointestinal hemorrhage" resulting from his liver disease. He also suffered from a "massively enlarged spleen" and some pulmonary edema. Ron "Pigpen" McKernan was dead at twenty-seven.

In 1979, Brent Mydland joined the band, replacing God-chaux and his wife, Donna, who had been singing with the band. On July 23, 1980, Keith Godchaux died from injuries suffered in a motorcycle accident. Almost ten years later to the day, on July 26, 1990, Mydland was dead from a drug overdose.

Drugs to Blame in Death of Blind Faith Bassist, Rick Grech

Rick Grech. (Courtesy ATCO Records)

RICK GRECH

The Grech family moved to Leicester in the 1950s from Bordeaux, France, where Rick Grech was born on November 1, 1945. Grech played violin in the city's youth symphony orchestra before joining an R&B band called the Farinas. The band changed their name to the Roaring Sixties, and finally to Family. Grech left Family on the eve of the group's U.S. tour and became one-quarter of the famous supergroup Blind Faith with Eric Clapton, Stevie Winwood, and Ginger Baker. Blind Faith released one LP before breaking up.

Grech then teamed up with Ginger Baker to form the group Ginger Baker's Air Force, but left in 1970 to join Winwood's group Traffic. Leaving in late 1971, Grech soon became an in-demand session player. Shifting activities to the United States, Grech coproduced *GP'73*, Gram Parson's solo debut album.

In 1973, Grech joined Clapton's all-star band for the Rainbow concert. Afterward, he joined forces with Mike Bloomfield and Carmon Appice in an effort to form another supergroup. This met with only moderate success, and Grech left in 1976 after the release of the LP *KGB*.

Over the years, Grech racked up credits with Rod Stewart, Muddy Waters, Viv Stanshall, and the Bee Gees and gained the respect of his peers in the music industry.

On March 17, 1990, Rick Grech died of physical debilities related to the longtime use of drugs. He was forty-four years old.

Spanky & Our Gang Guitarist Martin Hale Dead at 27

Spanky and Our Gang. (Courtesy Photofest)

MARTIN HALE

Taking their name from the 1930s comedy films, Spanky & Our Gang would chart five Top 40 hits between 1967 and 1968. The band consisted of Elaine "Spanky" McFarlane, Martin Hale, Kenny Hodges, Lefty Baker, Nigel Pickering, and John Seiter.

Their first LP, *Spanky & Our Gang*, brought them their highest-charting single, "Sunday Will Never Be the Same." The song stayed on the charts for five weeks, reaching No. 9. Many compared their sound and style to the Mamas and the Papas.

Like to Get to Know You, the name of their second LP, was also the title of their third Top 20 single. During the making of their third LP, *Without Rhyme or Reason*, Martin Hale unexpectedly died of cirrhosis in 1968. He was twenty-seven years old.

Hollywood

Hit Songwriter Dies of Drug Overdose

Tim Hardin.

TIM HARDIN

Widely known for his songwriting ability, Hardin penned hit songs for the Four Tops, Bobby Darin, Peter, Paul & Mary, Rod Stewart, and many others. Hardin began his career in music after being discharged from the U.S. Marines in the late fifties. Drifting into the folk circuit, Hardin was well received at the Newport Folk Festival in 1966 and released his solo LP *Tim Hardin* the same year.

Hardin wrote such classics as "If I Were a Carpenter," "Reason to Believe," and "Misty Roses," to name a few. Hardin moved to Woodstock in the late sixties, where it is rumored that he greatly influenced Bob Dylan's album *John Wesley Harding*.

Hardin settled in England in 1970 and released a number of LPs on different labels. Considered for the role of Woody Guthrie in the film *Bound for Glory* in 1976, Hardin returned to the United States, but didn't get the role. He was soon back in the studio and, while negotiating a new record deal with Polygram, died of a heroin overdose on December 29, 1980. Tim Hardin died less than a week after his thirty-ninth birthday.

Adie Harris, 42, Dead of a Heart Attack

The Shirelles. (Courtesy Rhino Records)

ADIE "MICKI" HARRIS

In junior high school, Adie "Micki" Harris, Shirley Owens, Beverly Lee, and Doris Kenner formed the Poquellos, which would become one of the most successful female vocal quartets of the early 1960s.

Schoolmate Mary Jean Greenberg was struck by the girls' talent and called her mother, record executive Florence Greenberg. After an audition, Greenberg signed the girls to her small Tiara record label in 1958, and the Shirells were born. The group released their first single, "I Met Him on a Sunday," the same year. It reached the Top 50 in the United States, and Decca soon gave the group a national distribution deal.

After Greenberg formed the Sceptor label, the group was back in the studio. Their 1959 release of "Dedicated to the One I Love" landed them in the Hot 100.

"Tonight's the Night," released in 1960, at No. 39, was their first song to break the Top 40 barrier. Also released in 1960, "Will You Love Me Tomorrow?"—written by Gerry Goffin and Carole King—catapulted up the charts, giving the group their first No. 1 single. To capitalize on their recent success, Sceptor reissued their 1959 recording of "Dedicated to the One I Love." The single stayed on the charts for fourteen weeks and reached the No. 3 position in 1961. "Mama Said," also released in 1961, gave the group their third Top 5 single in a row.

In 1962, the Shirelles charted five singles, including their No. 1 hit "Soldier Boy." But things started to wind down in 1963, when the group was able to chart only two more Top 40 records. These would be the last of the superhits for the group. By 1967, the Shirelles had all but vanished from the

Top 100. They re-formed in the seventies to perform in oldies shows.

On June 10, 1982, at the age of forty-two, Adie "Micki" Harris died of a heart attack.

Donny Hathaway Jumps 15 Floors to His Death

Donny Hathaway. (Courtesy Atlantic Records)

DONNY HATHAWAY

Donny Hathaway's singing career began at the age of three when he was billed as Donny Pitts, the Nation's Youngest Gospel Singer. He accompanied himself on the ukulele. Hathaway attended Howard University on a scholarship where he met classmate Roberta Flack, whom he would record with in later years.

Creating a name for himself by doing session work, Hathaway recorded with Jerry Butler, Carla Thomas, and the Staple Singers. Hathaway's big break came when he met King Curtis and was signed to Atlantic Records. His first LP, *Everything Is Everything*, released in 1970, included the minor hit "The Ghetto." Hathaway did not chart in the Top 40 until he began singing with Roberta Flack in 1971. Their first duet, "You Got a Friend," charted at No. 29. The next two were in the Top 10—"Where Is the Love" at No. 5 and "The Closer I Get to You" at No. 2.

By the mid-seventies Hathaway's career began a downward spiral due to personal problems. On January 13, 1979, deeply depressed, he jumped fifteen floors to his death.

London

Rock Star Jimi Hendrix Dead in London at 27

Jimi Hendrix. (Courtesy Carl Depola Photographer)

JIMI HENDRIX

The musicians of the sixties took their music far beyond the borders of a simple 4/4 beat. It was a time of hallucinogenic drugs and experimental music. Jimi Hendrix, born November 28, 1942, a high school dropout from Seattle, was called "the most pornographic of these performers." In his tight black pants and wild Afro hairdo, Jimi Hendrix played his Stratocaster guitar between his legs, on his back, and with his teeth, and on occasion he would set his guitar on fire at the end of a concert.

As with many other rock stars of the time, Jimi's drug problem was serious and public, and it grew worse as his fame grew. He would stay stoned for days on end. It started to affect his music, and by 1970 he was booed off stage when in the middle of a song he threw down his guitar and told the audience, "I just can't get it together."

He returned to London after a series of bad concerts and met up with girlfriend Monica Danneman. On the evening of September 17, 1970, they went to a party and later spent most of the early morning hours in a bar. Returning to a friend's flat at about seven the next morning, Monica took one of her prescription sleeping pills and put the remaining pills on the bedside table. Hendrix, unable to fall asleep, swallowed the remaining pills. Waking up at about ten-thirty A.M., Danneman left the room for a few minutes and, when she returned, noticed that Hendrix had vomited in his sleep. Although his heart was still beating, she couldn't wake him. Danneman called an ambulance and Hendrix was taken to a hospital where he died from suffocation of his own vomit.

Over the years many have suspected that Jimi Hendrix had committed suicide in light of his bad concerts, the recent rejection by fans, and financial pressures. Many others feel it was simply an unavoidable accident, due to his constant drug use. At his funeral, fellow musicians held a jam session and a seven-foot floral guitar was laid on his grave.

Iowa

Three Rock-'n'-Roll Stars Die in Iowa Air Crash

Buddy Holly.

BUDDY HOLLY

RITCHIE VALENS

J. P. RICHARDSON
(THE BIG BOPPER)

"The day the music died" is how many describe the death of Buddy Holly. Born Charles Hardin Holley in Lubbock, Texas, on September 7, 1936, Buddy Holly would set the tone of rock 'n' roll for everyone who followed. By the time he was twenty-one, Holly had written such classics as "That'll Be the Day" and "Peggy Sue" and had appeared on *The Ed Sullivan Show*. He had also toured England and Australia.

Selling records in those early days of rock 'n' roll meant a lot of travel and one-night stands. On February 2, 1959, Holly and other rock acts were on their way from Green Bay, Wisconsin, to Clear Lake, Iowa, where they were to perform that evening. The bus they were traveling on was unheated and the weather was bitter cold. The thought of traveling another three hundred miles to Moorhead, Minnesota, for their next show was unthinkable to Holly, Ritchie Valens, and J. P. "Big Bopper" Richardson. They decided to charter a small plane and fly to Moorhead after their evening show. It was about one A.M. when the three of them boarded the aircraft. The temperature was eighteen degrees with a light snow and thirty-five-mile-an-hour winds. Their twenty-one-year-old pilot was not certified to fly by instruments, something he would surely have to do in poor weather.

When the plane hadn't arrived the next morning, a search plane took off from the same airport to trace the missing plane's course. The plane was spotted only eight miles from the airport. Even though the plane had crashed in a cornfield just a few hundred yards from a farmhouse, nobody had heard the crash. Marks on the ground showed that the plane hit the ground, bounded fifty feet, then skidded five hundred feet before hitting a fence and breaking up. Buddy Holly was dead at age twenty-two, Ritchie Valens dead at seventeen, and the Big Bopper dead at age twenty-eight.

Englewood, New Jersey

Heart Attack Claims Life of O'Kelly Isley

The Isley Brothers.

O'KELLY ISLEY

On April 17, 1956, Ronald, Rudolph, and O'Kelly Isley boarded a Greyhound bus from their hometown of Cincinnati, Ohio, for New York City. Encouraged by their father, the Isley brothers had grown up singing and performing gospel music and were now on their way to the big time.

Once in New York, the Isleys made several records produced by a number of small independent labels. Between 1957 and early 1959, the Isleys were unable to produce a hit. They were, however, beginning to develop a strong stage show and soon signed with the booking-agent firm of General Artists Corp. RCA Records picked up their contract, and the brothers were soon recording on a major label.

On July 29, 1959, the Isley Brothers recorded what would be their first milestone, "Shout—Pts 1&2." Released as a single in August, "Shout" climbed to No. 47 on *Billboard's* Hot 100. Although the Isleys continued to record and release singles, it took nearly three years before they would chart a Top 40 single.

In 1962, now recording on the Wand label, the Isleys had their first Top 20 single with the release of "Twist and Shout." Produced by Phil Spector and Jerry Wexler, "Twist and Shout" topped the R&B charts before crossing over and climbing the pop charts to No. 17. Six months later, the song crossed the Atlantic. Heard by John Lennon, it was soon recorded by the Beatles and released as a single in 1964. The Beatles version of "Twist and Shout," charting at No. 2, was the Beatles' sixth entry into the pop Top 40.

On May 21, 1964, "Testify—Pts. 1 and 2" was recorded as a tribute to the Beatles, James Brown, Ray Charles, and Jackie Wilson; it was the first release on the brothers' own T-Neck label, with worldwide distribution handled by Atlantic Records. "Testify" also featured the guitar work of a young Jimmy James, who would become famous as Jimi Hendrix. Despite a lavish production, "Testify" was not a hit, and nearly two years passed before the Isleys charted again.

Signing with Motown in 1965, the Isley Brothers were soon recording songs written by the team of Holland/Dozier/Holland. "This Old Heart of Mine," released in 1966, was the trio's second Top 20 single. But this would be the last Top 40 release until the brothers left Motown and reactivated their own T-Neck label. The release of "It's Your Thing" in 1969 took the Isleys back up the charts to No. 2, their highest-charting single. In the next eleven years, the Isley Brothers charted another eight Top 40 singles.

On March 31, 1986, O'Kelly Isley suffered a fatal heart attack. He was forty-eight years old.

London

Brian Jones, 27, Dies

Guitarist-Singer With Rolling Stones Found Unconscious in Swimming Pool

The Rolling Stones. Brian Jones (second from left)

BRIAN JONES

Born Lewis Brian Hopkin-Jones on February 28, 1942, Brian Jones was to become an integral part of one of the greatest rock-'n'-roll bands in the history of rock music. After years of success as the handsome rhythm-guitar player of the Rolling Stones, Jones found himself lost and desperate in a new band that was slowly slipping away from him. As Jones began to fall further and further into drugs, alcohol, and depression, it was only a matter of time before his world would collapse.

On the evening of Wednesday, July 2, 1969, Jones and Anna Wohlin, his new girlfriend, were joined by friends Frank Thoroughgood and Janet Lawson for dinner. On this humid and cloudy night, Jones, who suffered from asthma and hayfever, was using his inhaler often. Feeling in limbo between leaving the Stones and forming his new band, he appeared to be in good spirits and a relaxed frame of mind. Frank Thoroughgood would later recall, "Brian wasn't really drunk, although he staggered slightly." Janet Lawson told police, "Brian had been drinking and taking sleeping pills."

At about ten-thirty on July 3, 1969, Jones invited Frank and Janet to join him and Anna for a swim. "I went to the pool to keep an eye on them" Janet said. "Brian had trouble getting on the diving board, so Frank helped him. The two men seemed a little sluggish, but I decided they could look after themselves." After about twenty minutes, Janet and Anna left the pool area and returned to the house. Ten minutes later Frank returned for a towel and a cigarette. At that point, Janet immediately returned to the pool to find Jones at the bottom motionless. Frank also returned to the pool, called for Anna, and they both dived in and pulled Jones out. Janet, who was a nurse, began CPR and massaged his heart. They phoned for an ambulance and a local doctor. When the ambulance arrived, they tried for about half an hour to revive him. When the local doctor finally arrived, he examined the body and pronounced Jones dead. Anna stated later that when they pulled Jones out of the water, he was still alive and had a pulse.

His inhaler was found at the edge of the pool; it wasn't clear whether his death was caused by a bad asthma attack, an epileptic fit, which Jones had suffered from on a number of occasions, or a lethal dose of pills and alcohol. Days later the coroner would report that Jones's death was caused by drowning under the influence of alcohol and drugs.

Brian Jones's funeral took place in the same church where he had been a choirboy in his native Cheltenham. Over half a million people gathered along the funeral route and outside the nine-hundred-year-old church to mourn his death.

Two books published in 1994 claim that Frank Thoroughgood, who died in November of 1993, confessed on his deathbed to murdering Brian Jones. Sussex police are reportedly looking into this new evidence.

Los Angeles

Rock Star Janis Joplin, 27, Found Dead in Hollywood

Janis Joplin. (Courtesy Herb Green)

JANIS JOPLIN

Janis Joplin was born in the small Texas town of Port Arthur on January 19, 1943. A rebellious youth, she left home in her early twenties and traveled to San Francisco where she sang in small clubs and coffeehouses. The drug and alcohol scene proved to be too much for Janis, and she soon returned home to Port Arthur.

In 1966, Big Brother and the Holding Company had already been playing together for about a year when they decided to add a female singer. Chet Helms, their manager at the time, suggested Joplin, a former college classmate at the University of Texas. Helms convinced Joplin to return to San Francisco and try out for the band.

The audition went well, and she signed on. The band played local gigs until they were booked for a month-long engagement in Chicago. This would be the turning point for the band. They played five to six sets a night, six nights a week, and developed a large following.

While in Chicago, they recorded their first album, *Big Brother and the Holding Company*. The album had a strong folk-rock feel to it, rather than the blues rock the band would later be known for.

Upon returning to the Bay area, Big Brother immediately played the Monterey Pop Festival. Here the band came to the attention of Columbia Records and was soon signed to the label. They would also change management, signing with New York manager Albert Grossman, who also handled Bob Dylan, Joan Baez, and Peter, Paul & Mary.

They soon started working on what would be known as their signature album, *Cheap Thrills*. The success of this album would give them worldwide acceptance, as well as establishing them as a major force in rock 'n' roll.

Before a second album could be recorded, Joplin decided to leave Big Brother and start her own band. Together with Sam Andrew, she put together the Kosmic Blues Band in December 1968. Alcohol and drugs became a permanent part of her life, and before long she and Sam Andrew were both addicted to heroin. Admitting that heroin helped her dull the fear of her newfound fame, Joplin predicted she would not live to the age of thirty. After about nine months with the Kosmic Blues Band, Sam Andrew decided to rejoin Big Brother.

After the departure of Andrew, the Kosmic Blues Band began to evolve into a new band called Full Tilt Boogie. In the fall of 1970, while working on her new album in Los Angeles, Joplin called City Hall to find out about a marriage license. She was happy, in love, and wanted to marry her latest boyfriend. Her work on the new album was phenomenal, and talk of a gold album was in the air.

On October 3, 1970, she called her supplier to get a fresh supply of heroin. She then went to the studio to work on her album, then out for a few drinks with friends. Returning to her hotel room at about midnight, she decided to shoot up some of her new heroin. The hotel clerk remembers her coming down to the lobby to get change for the cigarette machine. That was the last time she was seen alive. When she didn't show up for a recording session the next day, her band became worried. She was found dead that evening, collapsed on the floor of her room. The time of her death was put at one-forty A.M. Sunday. The cause of her death, an overdose of heroin.

Janis Joplin was cremated and her ashes were scattered along the Marin County coastline of California.

Chicago's Guitarist Terry Kath Blows His Brains Out

Terry Kath.

TERRY KATH

Originally know as the Big Thing, Chicago was formed in 1967 by Terry Kath, Peter Cetera, Robert Lamm, Denny Seraphine, Lee Loughmame, James Pankow, and Walt Parazaider. They soon changed their name to Chicago Transit Authority and released their first LP. After being sued by Chicago's Mayor Daley, the band shortened their name to Chicago. All but Lamm were native Chicagoans. Between 1970 and 1991, Chicago would have thirty-five songs in *Billboard*'s Top 40, with twenty of them in the Top 10 and three at No. 1.

With hits like "Make Me Smile," "25 or 6 to 4," and "Does Anybody Really Know What Time It Is?" Chicago became one of the most commercially successful groups in rock. They would top over $160 million in sales.

On the afternoon of January 23, 1978, Terry Kath attended a party in Woodland Hills, California, at the home of road-crew member Don Johnson. After the party broke up, only Kath remained there with Johnson. Kath, who had been drinking for most of the party, began twirling around an automatic pistol he had brought with him. When Johnson asked Kath to stop playing with the gun, Kath replied, "Don't worry, it's not loaded, see?" He put the gun to his head and pulled the trigger. Kath died instantly. The accident occurred just eight days before his thirty-second birthday.

Paul Kossoff Dies While in Flight From London to New York

Paul Kossoff. (Courtesy A&M Records)

PAUL KOSSOFF

Formed in London in 1968, Free consisted of vocalist Paul Rodgers, Paul Kossoff, Simon Kirke, and Andy Fraser. Originally with Black Cat Bones, Kossoff and Kirke recruited Rodgers from Brown Suger and Fraser from John Mayall's Bluesbreakers.

In 1968, Free released their first LP, entitled *Tons of Sobs*, and in 1969, the album *Free*. Neither album made much impact on the music scene. In 1970, the release of their third album, *Fire and Ice*, would bring the group sudden success, with the hit single "All Right Now" reaching No. 4 in the United States and No. 2 in the United Kingdom. Their follow-up LP, *Highway*, flopped in the United Kingdom. They released their last album, *Free Live*, before breaking up in 1971. Fans consider *Free Live* the essential Free album.

Kossoff and Rodgers then formed the group Peace, followed by Toby, but both groups were short-lived. Kossoff then joined Kirke, Tetsu Yamauchi, and Texan John "Rabbit" Bundrick to make an easygoing instrumental LP, after which there was a stormy, short-lived reunion of Free in 1972. Bundrick and Yamauchi now became part of Free's new lineup. The band broke up after Kossoff collasped onstage, the result of his drug addiction.

Rodgers and Kirke formed the band Bad Company, and Kossoff formed his own band, Back Street Crawler. While on a flight from London to New York on March 19, 1976, Paul Kossoff died from a drug-induced heart attack. He was twenty-five years old.

London

Ex–Lead Singer for Thin Lizzy Dead at 35

Phil Lynott. (Courtesy Mercury Records)

PHIL LYNOTT

Phil Lynott formed the Irish rock group Thin Lizzy in 1969 after learning to play bass while living on skid row. Consisting of Brian Downey, Eric Bell, and Lynott, the band was signed to Decca Records. Thin Lizzy made the charts in 1973 with the hit single "Whiskey in the Jam," which reached No. 6 in the United Kingdom.

After the departure of Bell, replacements, including Gary Moore, Andy Gee, and John Cann, came and went. When Brian Robertson and Scott Gorhan joined Thin Lizzy, the band landed a new record deal with Vertigo Records. But their LP *Nightlife and Fighting*, released in 1974, flopped. Two years passed before the band finally charted in the United States with the release of *Jailbreak* in 1976.

After the release of *Johnny the Fox* in 1977, Robertson left the band, then rejoined the following year to record *Live and Dangerous* before leaving for good. The group released the LP *Black Rose* in 1979; this LP topped the British charts with four hit singles.

After a few more personnel changes, and the release of *Thunder and Lighting* in 1983, Thin Lizzy disbanded. Lynott then decided to pursue his occasional solo career, having released *Solo in Solo* in 1980, followed by *The Phil Lynott Album* in 1982.

Lynott was taken to Salisbury Infirmary after he collapsed at his West London home on Christmas Day, 1985; he was treated for a kidney and liver infection. While in the intensive care unit, he developed pneumonia and died of heart failure on January 4, 1986, that was brought on by his infections. He was thirty-four years old.

Gillsburg, Mississippi
6 Killed in Plane Crash
Including 3 Members of the Lynyrd Skynyrd Rock Band

Lynyrd Skynyrd. (From left) Leon Wilkeson, Artimus Pyle, (from the top) Allen Collins, Billy Powell, Ronnie Van Zant, Gary Rossington, and Steve Gaines. (Courtesy MCA Records)

LYNYRD SKYNYRD

Ronnie Van Zant

Steven Gaines

Cassie Gaines

Allen Collins

As lead singer of the Southern rhythm-and-blues band Lynyrd Skynyrd, Ronnie Van Zant was part of one of the hottest acts of the mid-1970s. Performing with a Confederate flag as a backdrop, Lynyrd Skynyrd sold over 1 million copies each of their records, starting with their second album, which featured the hit song "Sweet Home Alabama."

On October 20, 1977, the band was flying over southern Mississippi when its chartered plane ran out of fuel and crashed in a wooded swamp near Gillsburg. Six of the twenty-six aboard the plane were killed. Ronnie Van Zant and two other band members—guitarist Steven Gaines and his sister, backing vocalist Cassie Gaines—were among them.

One of the survivors later said that the plane was in poor condition and that a week before the crash a six-foot flame shot out of one of the plane's two engines. Another survivor stated that just before the crash, oil poured out of one of the engines. The pilot, who was also killed in the crash, had told the band that the plane was to be worked on in Baton Rouge, Louisiana, its destination when it crashed.

One week earlier, the band had released its fourth album, *Street Survivors*, which pictured the band surrounded by flames. Five hundred thousand copies had already been sold when the crash occurred. The remaining copies were pulled and a new cover was designed.

In 1988, MCA released the double live album *For the Glory of the South*. On January 23, 1990, tragedy struck once again with the death of Allen Collins from a respiratory ailment.

Orlando

The Band's Richard Manuel Commits Suicide by Hanging

The Band. (From left) Richard Manuel, Rick Danko, Robbie Robertson, Garth Hudson, and Levon Helm. (Courtesy Warner Brothers)

RICHARD MANUEL

As the piano player and vocalist with the rock group The Band, Richard Manuel would share the stage with Bob Dylan, Eric Clapton, Neil Young, and many other rock-'n'-roll legends.

Originating in Canada, The Band consisted of Rick Danko, Robbie Robertson, Levon Helm, Garth Hudson, and Richard Manuel. In 1965, The Band was hired to back Bob Dylan on his first all-electric world tour. This lasted until July 1966, when Dylan had his near-fatal motorcycle accident. Both Dylan and The Band retired to the rural house Big Pink, near Woodstock, New York, where The Band started rehearsing new songs that resulted in rock's first important bootleg. *Great White Wonder* would later be released by Columbia Records as *The Basement Tapes*

With word-of-mouth PR and rumors from George Harrison and Eric Clapton, fans anxiously awaited the release of The Band's debut album, *Music From Big Pink*, which featured the instant classic "The Weight." In 1969, they released their second album, *The Band*, which included "Up on Cripple Creek" and "The Night They Drove Old Dixie Down." Their third album, *Stage Fright*, was released in 1970. Three more albums were released between 1970 and 1973. During 1973, The Band played to over six hundred thousand fans at the history-making Watkins Glen Festival.

By 1976, after sixteen years on the road, The Band decided to call it quits. They played one last massive gig on Thanksgiving Day at Winterland, San Francisco. The show was filmed by director Martin Scorsese and included appearances by Clapton, Dylan, Ringo Starr, and many other friends of the band. The film and a three-disc album were released as *The Last Waltz*

Between 1983 and 1986, The Band played a number of reunion shows. It was after a sold-out show in Winter Park, a suburb of Orlando, Florida, that Richard Manuel was found on March 4, 1986 by his wife, hanged in the bathroom of his hotel room. The coroner labeled the death a suicide, although Manuel did not leave a note. He died one month shy of his forty-third birthday.

Fire Takes the Life of Rock Star Steve Marriott

Humble Pie. (From left) Jerry Shirley, Bobby Tench, Steve Marriott, Anthony "Sooty" Jones. (Courtesy ATCO Records)

STEVE MARRIOTT

Steve Marriott, born in London on January 30, 1947, was a child actor at the age of twelve. He released his first solo single, "Give Her My Regards," when he was sixteen and formed his first group, Steve Marriott's Moments, soon after.

In 1965, together with Ronnie Lane, Kenney Jones, and Ian McLagen, Marriott formed the now-legendary Small Faces. "Itchycoo Park," released in 1968, would be their highest-charting song in the United States. The group disbanded in 1969, and Marriott joined forces with Peter Frampton, Greg Ridley, and Jerry Shirley to form Humble Pie.

With the departure of Frampton in 1971, Marriott moved the band into heavy metal with the release of the LP *Smokin'*. Finding little reward in that direction, Marriott gravitated toward soul, adding black female vocalists Clydie King, Venetta Fields, and Billie Barnum. The two-disc live/studio album *Eat It* was released in 1973. Two more albums were released before the group disbanded in 1975. Two short-lived reunions took place—one in 1976 with Small Faces and one in 1980 with Humble Pie.

The 1980s found Marriott playing the London pub circuit in a band called Packet of Three. But the nineties began promisingly. Marriott and Frampton were back together working on a new album. Five songs were already recorded when Marriott decided to take a break and fly home to London, a journey from which he would never return. On April 20, 1991, Steve Marriott became the victim of an accidental fire at his home in London. He was forty-four years old.

Heart Failure Claims the Life of Ex-Wings Guitarist Jimmy McCulloch

Jimmy McCulloch.

JIMMY McCULLOCH

Originally the guitarist with Thunderclap Newman, by 1975 McCulloch was playing in Paul McCartney's supergroup Wings. Wings would chart two No. 1 hits and four others in the Top 40 before his departure in 1977.

Born in Glasgow on August 13, 1953, McCulloch was considered a guitar prodigy. In the late sixties when The Who's guitarist Pete Townshend helped fellow musicians John "Speedy" Keen and Andy Newman put together a new band, they recruited McCulloch and Thunderclap Newman was born. The group's first release, "Something in the Air," was a surprise No. 1 single in the United Kingdom in 1969. The song was also used in the film *The Magic Christian*. With the addition of Jim Avory, replacing Townshend, who sat in on bass, and Jimmy's younger brother Jack on drums, the band started touring.

With their second release, "Accidents," just missing the Top 40 and most of their live gigs not producing a large turnout, the band started to fade. Townshend produced one last album, *Hollywood Dream* in 1970. Soon after, the band broke up.

McCulloch, now a journeyman guitarist, played with the likes of John Mayall, Stone the Crows, Blue, Wings, and finally the Dukes. On September 27, 1979, McCulloch died of heart failure. Many suspect his death was due in part to drugs.

Drugs Involved in Death of Rock Star Robbie McIntosh

Average White Band. (Courtesy Atlantic Records)

ROBBIE McINTOSH

Formed in Scotland in 1972, the Average White Band consisted of Alan Gorrie, Hamish Stuart, Onnie McIntosh, Malcolm Duncan, Roger Ball, and Robbie McIntosh. Naming themselves after their obsession with black music, the group came to the attention of the public while on tour as the warm-up band for Eric Clapton's Rainbow Theatre comeback concert in 1973.

After a slow start with their first album, *Show Your Hand*, released in 1973 on MCA, the band changed their record company as well as their producer. As a result of these changes, their second album, *AWB*, released in 1974 on Atlantic, reached No. 1. Their disco instrumental single "Pick Up the Pieces" also reached No. 1 in America and No. 6 in the United Kingdom. But success would be short-lived for Robbie McIntosh. On September 23, 1974, he died from a drug overdose at age twenty-four.

London

British Rock Star Freddie Mercury Dies of AIDS

Freddie Mercury.

FREDDIE MERCURY

Born Frederick Bulsara in Zanzibar on September 5, 1946, Freddie Mercury would become one of the most flamboyant figures in rock 'n' roll. With Mercury, Brian May, John Deacon, and Roger Taylor, Queen charted thirteen Top 40 singles including two number ones, two gold, and two platinum. They also released nineteen albums, with eight of them reaching No. 1.

Originally recording as Larry Lurex, Mercury joined up with May and Taylor after the demise of their band Smile in 1971. Deacon was recruited after he replied to an advertisement in the music press. Signed to a lucrative contract with EMI, they flopped with their first single, "Keep Yourself Alive." Their first album was released in 1973. The band began to grow in popularity while on tour with Mott the Hoople and was on the way to becoming one of the most popular rock groups of the 1970s.

Their following grew in 1974 with the release of two albums, *Queen II* and *Sheer Heart Attack*. The group was now receiving critical acclaim from the rock press for their aggressive rock and ingenious arrangements. Their fifth single, "Killer Queen," landed the group their first Top 20 single, reaching No. 12. "Killer Queen" stayed on the charts for eleven weeks.

Near the end of 1975, one of the most extravagant and expensive albums of the era was released. *A Night at the Opera*, with its elaborate production of "Bohemian Rhapsody," instantly established the group in the top echelon of rock 'n' roll. For the next eight years, Queen continued to produce chart-topping hits. Their 1980 release of "A Little Thing Called Love" remained on the charts for seventeen weeks, reaching No. 1. Their following release, "Another One Bites the Dust," also reached No. 1 and stayed on the charts for twenty-one weeks.

In 1991, after wide speculation about Mercury's failing health, the group surprised the world with the release of *Innuendo*. The album debuted at No. 1 in the United Kingdom. This would be the last album of new material released while Mercury was alive. On November 23, 1991, he announced to the world that he had contracted AIDS. He died the next day.

Trying to increase public awareness of AIDS, Mercury called on his fans from around the world to join in the fight against the disease. He was forty-five years old.

Keith Moon, Drummer for The Who, Found Dead in His London Flat

Keith Moon. (Courtesy Rhino Records)

KEITH MOON

Known for his excessive drinking and heavy drug use, Keith Moon actually died from the very drug prescribed to help him beat his alcoholism.

With a group originally called the High Numbers, which soon became The Who, Moon joined Peter Townshend, Roger Daltrey, and John Entwhistle on a journey that would take them to the peak of the rock-'n'-roll world. As The Who, the band started to develop their famous stage show, which included the destroying of their instruments at its end. The Who's big break came with the release of "My Generation," which topped the British charts at No. 2. After an explosive appearance at the Monterey Pop Festival, The Who established themselves as a leading rock-'n'-roll act in the United States. From 1967 to 1982, The Who would have sixteen Top 40 songs on the U.S. charts, and in 1990 they were admitted to the Rock 'n' Roll Hall of Fame.

After living in Los Angeles for some time, Moon decided to return to London around the middle of 1976. According to Bill Curbishley, The Who's manager, Moon was off booze and drugs and was starting a fitness routine to get back in shape. The Who were about to embark on another world tour, and Curbishley had just completed a two-movie deal with the Polygram Group.

On the evening of September 6, 1978, Moon had cocktails and dinner with Paul McCartney and some other friends, who all attended the London premier of *The Buddy Holly Story*. Upon returning home, Moon took some Heneneverin pills prescribed by his doctor to help get him through the withdrawal effects of alcoholism. He then went to bed and woke up about two hours later in a dazed and confused state.

According to his girlfriend, he then took more Heneneverin pills and went back to sleep, a sleep from which he never woke up.

The coroner reported the cause of death as an accidental overdose of Heneneverin. Apparently, due to the large dinner Moon had consumed earlier, the first pills he had taken were slow to enter his system. After taking the second lot of pills, the two combined to create a lethal overdose. Another tragic accident, which took the life of one of the rock world's greatest drummers. He was thirty-one years old.

Paris

Jim Morrison, 27, Lead Singer With The Doors, Dies in Bath

Jim Morrison. (Courtesy Elektra Entertainment)

JIM MORRISON

Three years after he dropped out of the UCLA film school, Jim Morrison became the lead singer of The Doors, one of America's most popular bands. He was known for his sexually suggestive lyrics and would become one of rock 'n' roll's most prolific songwriters of the late 1960s.

Morrison had a problem with drinking and drugs from the beginning. At first it was an integral part of his image, but by 1969 his drug habit was out of control. He verbally abused and spit on his fans. He constantly got busted for drunkenness and was once arrested for exposing himself onstage. During tours he would hang off the balcony of his hotel room, just for the thrill of it. The Doors' manager, Danny Sugarman, remembers that Morrison's outrageous image always overshadowed his poetry and music.

Fed up with problems and legal hassles from his record company, Morrison decided a change of scenery would do him good. He was determined to get back to his poetry and stop drinking. So, in March 1971, Morrison and Pamela Courson, his longtime girlfriend, left for Paris. Rather than work seriously on his poetry, Morrison often stayed out all night drinking and getting high. He once said, referring to Hendrix and Joplin, "You're drinking with number three."

After having dinner out on Friday, July 2, Morrison took Pamela home and decided to see a movie alone. The events that took place after this remain a mystery. In the early hours of the morning, Morrison returned home and apparently suffered a heart attack while taking a bath. Rumors of Morrison's death began to surface. On Monday, July 5, when an Elektra Records executive called Courson to verify the rumor, he was told he should come to Paris. Upon arriving in Paris on Tuesday, the Elektra representative found Courson with a sealed coffin and a death certificate stating that Morrison had died of a heart attack at twenty-eight years of age. Morrison was buried the next day.

Questions still surround Jim Morrison's death. Why was the official announcement not made until Thursday, July 8? What had actually happened between July 2 and July 5? Did Morrison go to a movie or did he go drinking instead? Courson said she woke up at 5 A.M. Saturday to find Morrison dead of a heroin overdose even though he wasn't known as a user. Others think he was killed as part of a conspiracy. And some insist that Jim Morrison never died at all. An unconfirmed report says he was seen boarding an airplane that weekend.

Dallas

Fiery Plane Crash Takes Life of Rock-'n'-Roll Legend Rick Nelson

Rick Nelson.

RICK NELSON

With the success of their 1952–66 television show, *The Adventures of Ozzie & Harriet*, the Nelson family entertained millions of households. In 1957, young Ricky Nelson became an instant rock star and teen idol when he performed a version of Fats Domino's "I'm Walkin'." And before his career had run its course, eighteen of his singles would be two-sided hits and nineteen singles would be in the Top 10.

With the start of the British Invasion in 1964 Nelson's popularity started to fade. He would not chart again until he formed his new band, Rick Nelson & the Stone Canyon Band, in 1969. His 1970 release of Bob Dylan's "She Belongs to Me" put Nelson back on the charts at No. 33. Two years later, he scored a Top 10 single and a gold-record award with "Garden Party."

On December 31, 1985, Nelson, his fiancée, Helen Blair, and five others were killed in the crash of their private DC-3 while en route to a New Year's Eve concert in Dallas. The plane crashed after the passenger cabin caught fire. Many believe the fire was started after one of the passengers freebased cocaine. Only the pilot and copilot survived the crash. Nelson was forty-five years old.

Rick Nelson was inducted into the Rock 'n' Roll Hall of Fame in 1987. His daughter, Tracy, is a film/TV actress, and his twin sons began recording in 1990.

London

Murcia of Dolls, Dead of Overdose

New York Dolls.

NEW YORK DOLLS

Billy Murcia

Johnny Thunders

Formed in London in 1971, the New York Dolls consisted of Johnny Thunders (John Genzale), Rick Rivets, Arthur Kane, Billy Murcia, and David Johanson. With Johanson's Mick Jagger–like style, it wasn't long before the New York Dolls started to attract a large following. On the road most of 1972, the group returned to London to start a U.K. tour, a tour from which Billy Murcia would never return. Heavily into alcohol and drugs, Murcia died of a heroin overdose on November 6, 1972, at the age of twenty-one.

Following Murcia's death, Rivets left the band. The Dolls then recruited Jerry Nolan to replace Murcia, and Sylvain Sylvain to replace Rivets. Signing with Mercury Records, the group was soon in the studio working on their debut album, *New York Dolls*, which was released in 1973. Most critics considered the album too amateurish.

They then changed producers and recorded their 1974 release, *Too Much Too Soon*. Mercury, however, dropped the band because of moderate sales. Switching managers, they were now under the wing of Malcom McLaren. But the band was unwilling to adopt McLaren's "red leather and Soviet flag" image. McLaren dropped the Dolls and returned to London.

Thunders and Nolan soon left and formed the Heartbreakers. Aligning themselves with U.K. punk rock, they released *LAMF* in 1977 and *Live At Max's Kansas City* in 1979. But sources close to Thunders stated that the rockers' lifestyle was beginning to take its toll. Thunders was diagnosed with leukemia and his body was deteriorating rapidly. But in the end an overdose of heroin would be Thunders's demise. He died on April 23, 1991.

Agoura Hills, California

Heart Attack Claims Life of Singer, Songwriter Harry Nilsson

Harry Nilsson.

HARRY NILSSON

Born Harry Edward Nelson III in Brooklyn, New York, on June 15, 1941, Nilsson moved with his family to California in 1958. After high school, he worked in the computer depart-ment of a bank in the San Fernando Valley. Nilsson wrote songs in his spare time and landed a contract with RCA Records in 1967. He was soon turning out hits for such artists was the Monkees, Three Dog Night, and the Yardbirds.

Nilsson's debut LP, *The Pandemonium Shadow Show*, received mixed reviews and was a slow seller. His second LP, *Aerial Ballet*, released in 1968, produced his first Top 10 sin-gle along with a Grammy for the theme song from the movie *Midnight Cowboy*. "Everybody's Talkin' " reached the No. 6 position on *Billboard*'s Top 40 on September 6, 1969.

His next two singles, "I Guess the Lord Must Be Living in New York City" and "Me and My Arrow" never climbed above No. 34. It was his 1972 release "Without You," written by Badfinger's Pete Ham and Tom Evans, that gave Nilsson his only No. 1 single. Between April of 1972 and May of 1974, Nilsson charted his last four singles. "Coconut" would be the only one to make the Top 10. The other three charted at Nos. 23, 27, and 39.

Turning to business interests in the 1980s, Nilsson was the CEO of Hawkeye Entertainment, a film, television, and music production company that he helped start. He had also recent-ly completed work on a new album while recovering from a massive heart attack he'd suffered on Valentine's Day 1993. At about four in the morning of January 15, 1994, Nilsson died in his sleep at his Agoura Hills, California, home. He was fifty-two years old.

New York

Singer-Songwriter Phil Ochs Hangs Himself at Sister's House in Queens

Phil Ochs. (Courtesy Rhino Records)

PHIL OCHS

The Ochs family moved to New York City from El Paso, Texas, when Phil Ochs was two years old. Drawn to the folk protest movement in 1961, Ochs came to be known as the "troubadour of the New Left." His songwriting would be compared to that of Bob Dylan. However, while Dylan's innovative style found a new audience, Ochs was content playing traditional folk-protest, saying he wanted to be "the first left-wing star." Unlike Dylan and many other folk artists of the time, Ochs never charted a single song in *Billboard*'s top 40.

"I Ain't Marching Anymore," released in 1963, was Ochs's first protest song of the Vietnam War era. "Talking Cuban Crisis" and "50 Mile Hike" were among the songs he frequently played in the Greenwich Village coffeehouses in the early sixties. In 1965, Joan Baez recorded his "There but for Fortune." The song would be her only Top 50 single that decade.

Ochs left the United States in the early seventies and traveled around Europe. He wrote for London's *Time Out* magazine before traveling to Africa, where he narrowly escaped death when he was mysteriously assaulted. Suffering from severely damaged vocal chords as a result of his attack, Ochs drifted deeply into alcohol and experienced extreme bouts of depression. He changed his name to John Butler Train and refused to answer to the name Phil Ochs. On April 9, 1976, Ochs committed suicide by hanging himself at his sister's house in Queens where he had been staying since December. He was thirty-five years old.

Hendersonville

Death of a Legend
Roy Orbison Dead at 52

Roy Orbison. (Courtesy Virgin Records, James Schnepf)

ROY ORBISON

Between 1960 and 1966, Roy Orbison would chart twenty-three songs in the Top 40. Born in Vernon, Texas, Orbison began his music career in 1952 with the creation of his first dance band, the Wink Westerners. His next band, the Teen Kings, was formed in 1954 and in 1956 released a remake of "Ooby Dooby" on Sun Records. The song charted No. 59, but the band soon broke up after an unsuccessful follow-up single.

Orbison then went to work as a house songwriter for Acuff-Rose in Nashville. But he was soon back in the recording studio after signing a record deal, first with RCA and then with Monument, where he would stay until 1965. His first two records with Monument flopped, but his third, released in 1960, "Only the Lonely," reached No. 2 in the United States and No. 1 in the United Kingdom. Over the next four years, Orbison had fourteen Top 40 hits, including his most notable No. 1 single, "Oh, Pretty Woman." After Orbison left Monument, he started recording for MGM.

On June 7, 1966, Orbison's wife, Claudette, was tragically killed in a motorcycle accident, and two years later a fire claimed the lives of two of his sons. Orbison would not resurface until 1985.

Inducted into the Rock 'n' Roll Hall of Fame in 1987, Orbison soon became a member of the supergroup the Traveling Wilburys. And in 1989, he charted posthumously at No. 9 with the hit song "You Got It" from his *Mystery Girl* LP.

On December 6, 1988, after spending the day with friends, Orbison suffered a massive heart attack. He was taken by ambulance to a nearby hospital in Hendersonville, Tennessee, where he died late that night. Elvis Presley once called Orbison "the greatest rock-'n'-roll singer in the world." Roy Orbison was fifty-two years old at the time of his death.

New York

Felix Pappalardi Found Murdered

Wife in Custody

Felix Pappalardi. (Courtesy Archive Records)

FELIX PAPPALARDI

After graduating from the Michigan Conservatory of Music, Felix Pappalardi joined the Greenwich Village folk scene, playing bass for singer Tim Hardin. Before long, Pappalardi made a name for himself as an arranger and producer. In 1967, he produced the Youngbloods as well as the supergroup Cream.

During a recording session for a band called the Vagrants, Pappalardi met their lead guitarist, Leslie West. Impressed by West's intuitive style, Pappalardi was soon producing West's first solo LP, entitled *Mountain*. Pappalardi, back on bass, and West recruited drummer Norman Smart and keyboard player Steve Knight. Taking the name of West's solo album, Mountain was soon in the studio recording their first album, *Mountain Climbing*. "Mississippi Queen," their first single from the album, landed the group on the charts at a respectable No. 21.

After the release of their second album, *Nantucket Sleighride*, in 1971, Norman Smart left the band and was replaced by Corky Laing. *Flowers of Evil* was soon released, followed by *Mountain Live* in 1972. Later that year, Mountain split up.

West and Laing joined forces with ex-Cream bassist Jack Bruce and formed the band West, while Pappalardi concentrated on a solo career. Traveling to Japan in 1976, Pappalardi produced the album *Felix Pappalardi and Creation*, and in 1978 he produced the punk band Dead Boys.

On April 17, 1983, Felix Pappalardi was found shot to death at his home in New York. His wife, Gail Collins, was taken into custody and charged with Pappalardi's murder. Felix Pappalardi was forty-four years old.

Los Angeles

Mysterious Death of Jeff Porcaro

Toto. Jeff Porcaro (bottom). (Courtesy Sony Music)

JEFF PORCARO

Formed in Los Angeles in 1978 and named after the dog in *The Wizard of Oz*, the group Toto consisted of Hartford-born Jeff Porcaro, his brother Steve, David Paich, David Hungate, Steve Lukather, and Bobby Kimball. The members were all top session players, who had worked with Aretha Franklin, Boz Scaggs, Steely Dan, Jackson Browne, Earth, Wind and Fire, and countless others.

Their first album, *Toto*, released in 1978, would stay on the charts for most of 1979. The album also produced three hit singles. "Hold the Line" was their first Top 10 single, climbing up the charts to No. 5 in November 1978. Their second and third albums, *Hydra* and *Turn Back*, received little success. Their only single to reach the Top 40 during this period was "99."

The release of *Toto IV* in 1982 turned things around for the band. The album skyrocketed to the top of the charts and produced another three hit singles. "Rosanna" gave the group their first No. 2, followed by "Africa," their first No. 1 hit single. Toto dominated the 1983 Grammy Awards, winning seven Grammys.

David Hungate left the group in 1983. He was replaced by a third Porcaro brother, Mike. The following year, Kimball left to pursue a solo career. He was replaced by ex–Trillion vocalist Fergie Frederiksen, who would remain in the group for two years before being replaced by Joseph Williams in 1986. Reforming after a two-year absence, Toto struggled to regain their previous success. The *Seventh One* was released in 1988.

In August 1992, after recording a new album, Toto was preparing to embark on a European tour. According to Jeff's father, Joe, Jeff got sick after he spent an afternoon spraying his garden with a chemical poison. Shortly before dinner, after taking a shower, Jeff complained to his wife that he wasn't feeling well. He soon developed a bad case of diarrhea and was taken to a hospital for observation. As doctors tried to diagnose his ailment, his condition worsened. Jeff Porcaro was pronounced dead on August 5, 1992. An autopsy revealed cocaine in his system. But, according to his father, it wasn't the cocaine or the poison that killed them. Jeff had actually died from hardening of the arteries.

Atlanta

Car Crash Kills Soul Singer Dave Prater of Sam and Dave

Sam and Dave. Dave Prater (right). (Courtesy Rhino
Records)

DAVE PRATER

When Dave Prater joined Sam Moore onstage in Miami in 1958, the legendary soul vocal duo of Sam and Dave was born. Sam, originally from Miami, and Dave, from Ocilla, Georgia, were signed to Roulette Records in 1960. When they failed to produce a hit for the label, they switched to Stax, a division of Atlantic Records. Working with Isaac Hayes and David Porter with the Memphis Horns, Sam and Dave recorded some of the best-loved hits of the soul era.

Reaching No. 1 on the soul charts and No. 21 on the pop charts, "Hold On! I'm Comin'," released in 1966, was the first in a series of hits for the duo. "Soul Man," released in 1967, gave them their second No. 1 on the soul charts and an incredible No. 2 on the pop charts. They scored once more in the pop Top 40 with "I Thank You," released in 1968 (No. 4 soul, No. 7 pop).

Switching to the parent Atlantic Records when Stax was sold in 1968, the duo released "Soul Sister, Brown Sugar." Reaching No. 18 on the soul charts, the song hit only No. 41 on the pop charts. In 1970, Sam and Dave split up. They reunited in 1971, but not being able to produce a hit, they again split up.

On April 9, 1988, Dave Prater was killed when the car he was driving went off the road on Interstate 75 near Sycamore, Georgia, and slammed into a tree. Dave Prater was fifty years old at the time of his death.

Memphis

The King Is Dead

Elvis Presley. (Courtesy RCA Records)

ELVIS PRESLEY

The King Is Dead. This was the headline when the undisputed King of Rock 'n' Roll was found unconscious in the bathroom of Graceland, his Memphis mansion. Between 1956 and 1977, Elvis received three Grammy Awards, three RIAA Platinum Record Awards, thirty-five RIAA Gold Record Awards, and had a total of one hundred and six Top 40 hits. He also appeared in thirty-three films.

After his divorce from his wife, Priscilla, in 1973, Presley's career started to go downhill. He constantly worried about his image and started dieting and taking pills to lose weight. Bad habits that he had developed early in his career were difficult to change. Staying up all night and sleeping all day gave his life no real pattern or structure. Elvis was found unconscious on his bathroom floor by his girlfriend, Ginger Alden. It was later disclosed he had been lying there for about three hours before Alden discovered him. Help was summoned, but all attempts to revive him were futile. His personal physician, Dr. George Nichopoulos, pronounced him dead at three-thirty P.M. on August 16, 1977, at a Memphis hospital.

No evidence of any illegal drugs was found at his home. There were, however, many drugs prescribed by his doctor. Elvis had suffered "cardiac arrhythmia" (irregular heartbeat) brought on by "undetermined causes." He would be ruled dead "by natural causes." Tens of thousands of people gathered outside his Memphis mansion to pay their last respects to the King of Rock 'n' Roll. Elvis Presley was inducted into the Rock 'n' Roll Hall of Fame in 1986. He was forty-two years old at the time of his death.

Parker, Arizona

Suicide Takes Life of Pop Singer Danny Rapp

Danny and the Juniors. (Courtesy Photofest)

DANNY RAPP

Formed in Philadelphia in 1955, Danny and the Juniors charted four Top 40 hits. "At the Hop," released in 1957, reached No. 1 and stayed on the charts for eighteen weeks. Their follow-up, "Rock and Roll Is Here to Stay," charted at No. 19, while "Dottie," released in 1958, and "Twistin' USA," released in 1960, didn't break the Top 20 mark. During the early sixties the group could be seen on the TV dance show *American Bandstand*.

Although the group had a No. 1 single and three other songs in the Top 40, few royalties were ever paid to them. The group started lawsuits to try to collect the back royalties due them. These suits would go on for years. For Danny Rapp, the wait was too long, and on April 8, 1983, his body was found in a motel room in Arizona. Another suicide brought on by the dark side of the music business. He was forty-one years old at the time of his death.

Madison

Otis Redding Feared Dead

Plane Crashes Into Lake Monona

Otis Redding. (Courtesy Atlantic Records)

OTIS REDDING

Born in Dawson, Georgia on September 9, 1941, Otis Redding spent most of his childhood in Macon. His musical influences included Little Richard, Ray Charles, and Sam Cooke. While working with Johnny Jenkins and the Pinetoppers in 1962, Redding recorded a demo that would launch his own solo career.

His appeal at first was mostly to the black audience. But in 1965 the Rolling Stones produced their album *Out of Our Heads*, incorporating the music of Redding, which clearly showed the importance of soul music to rock 'n' roll. In 1967, Aretha Franklin recorded Redding's composition "Respect," sending it to the top of the pop charts. As a thank-you to the Rolling Stones, Redding recorded his own version of the Stones' hit "Satisfaction."

Touring Europe in 1966 and 1967, Redding became a tremendous hit and was voted the number one male vocalist by *Melody Maker* magazine, ousting Elvis, who had held this honor for the past ten years. Redding's composition "Dock of the Bay" became his biggest hit, but only posthumously. Recorded two months before his death, "Dock of the Bay" stayed on the charts for almost a year.

On December 10, 1967, Otis and his band were on their way to an engagement in the Midwest. Rain and heavy fog had settled in when their plane started an instrument landing. The plane was three miles from the airport when it crashed into Lake Monona. One person survived, but Redding and four others drowned. More than four thousand people jammed into the Macon Auditorium while another three thousand stood outside for the funeral service.

London

Freak Accident Kills Ex-Yardbird Keith Relf

Keith Relf (second from right, top).

KEITH RELF

As the lead singer of the legendary British rock group the Yardbirds, Keith Relf would share the stage with the likes of Eric Clapton, Jeff Beck, and Jimmy Page.

Originally formed as the Metropolitan Blues Quartet, the band consisted of Keith Relf, Anthony Topham, Chris Dreja, Paul Samwell-Smith, and Jim McCarty. When Topham left the group in 1963, he was replaced by Eric Clapton. In 1965, Eric Clapton left the group and was replaced by Jeff Beck. Jimmy Page joined the group in 1966 replacing Samwell-Smith. Later the same year Jeff Beck left the group. Between 1965 and 1968, The Yardbirds had five hit songs in the Top 20 and one in the Top 30. "For Your Love," released in 1965, would be their highest-charting release at No. 6 for nine weeks. Other hits included "Heart Full of Soul," "I'm a Man," "Shape of Things," and "Over Under Sideways Down." The Yardbirds disbanded in July 1968. Keith Relf and Jim McCarty formed Renaissance in 1969, which included Relf's sister Jane, before playing with Medicine Head and forming the short-lived Armageddon in 1975.

On May 14, 1976, Keith Relf was found dead in his West London home, from an apparent electrocution. His guitar amplifier was still switched on and his electric guitar lay next to his body. Relf was forming a new group called Illusion with his sister and McCarty when the fatal accident occurred. Keith Relf was thirty-three years old.

Los Angeles

Singer Minnie Riperton Dies of Cancer

Minnie Riperton. (Courtesy Michael Putland/Retna)

MINNIE RIPERTON

Minnie Riperton, born in Chicago on November 8, 1947, worked as a receptionist at Chess Records before recording under the name Andrea Davis in 1966 for the Chess label. Between 1967 and 1970, Riperton, with her incredible five-and-a-half-octive range, was the lead singer in the rock-R&B band Rotary Connection. The group released two albums in 1968. After leaving the group, Riperton began touring with Roberta Flack, Quincy Jones, and with Stevie Wonder's back-up group, Wonderlove, in 1973.

After Riperton signed with Epic Records, her first album, *Perfect Angel*, produced by Stevie Wonder, charted at No. 4 and included the No. 1 single "Lovin' You," cowritten with her husband, Dicky Rudolph. *Adventure in Paradise*, released in 1975, charted in the Top 20 LPs, but did not produce a second Top 40 single. After the release of *Stay in Love* in 1977, Riperton signed with Capitol Records. Her first album for Capitol, called *Minnie*, released in 1979, charted in the Top 30 LPs. Minnie Riperton's career was cut tragically short when she died from cancer on July 12, 1979.

Alcohol Binge Kills AC/DC Lead Singer, Bon Scott

AC/DC. Bon Scott (second from right)

BON SCOTT

Formed in Australia in 1974, the original AC/DC lineup consisted of Ronald Belford "Bon" Scott, Angus Young, Malcolm Young, Phil Rudd, and Mark Evans. The Youngs' older brother, George, a former member of the rock band the Easybeats, helped AC/DC obtain a recording contract. They released two albums in 1975, *High Voltage* and *TNT*. By 1976, the band had their first U.S./U.K. release.

They gained popularity by their outrageous stage show, which included Angus Young dressing like a schoolboy in short trousers. *Let There Be Rock*, released in 1977, would reach the Top 20 in the British charts. Soon after, bass player Mark Evans left the band and was replaced by Cliff Williams. They then released the LP *Powerage* in 1978.

As superstars on the heavy-metal circuit, AC/DC helped break down the wall that had isolated Australian rock from the mainstream. One of their best-known albums, *Highway to Hell*, released in 1979, made a strong showing in the United States. But the group's biggest success would come only after the death of Bon Scott.

On February 19, 1980, after appearing at Camden Town's Music Machine in London, Bon Scott died in his car after an evening of binge drinking. The coroner reported that he "drank himself to death." Bon Scott was thirty-three years old.

Santa Clarita

Singer-Songwriter of the '60s Takes His Own Life

Del Shannon. (Courtesy Rhino Records)

DEL SHANNON

Born Charles Westover in Coopersville, Michigan on December 30, 1939, Shannon spent his days working in a carpet store while developing his craft playing and singing in local clubs at night. Emerging onto the pop music scene in 1961 as Del Shannon, he recorded one of the era's most distinctive songs, "Runaway." Featuring his poignant falsetto and haunting Musitron organ lead, "Runaway" would take Shannon to the top of the charts, reaching No. 1 in both the United States and the United Kingdom.

Between 1961 and 1965, Shannon had eight Top 40 hits, including "Hats Off to Harry" and "Keep Searchin' (We'll Follow the Sun)." He also wrote the hit song "I Go to Pieces," recorded by Peter & Gordon.

Shannon fell from favor with record producers over a series of lawsuits regarding royalties, and record companies began to shy away from him for fear of being sued. According to Shannon, "I'd had a string of hits, but I couldn't record. I was so frustrated I'd go out and play golf in the snow. When I was twenty, I was drinking, and when I was thirty, I was drinking more, and when I was forty, I was drinking way too much." It wasn't until 1982 that Shannon hit the charts again. "Sea of Love," produced by Tom Petty, charted at No. 33 for four weeks.

Although he quit drinking in 1979, Shannon suffered from bouts of depression. During 1989, Shannon was considered a possible replacement for Roy Orbison, who had died the year before, in the Traveling Wilburys. He was also nearing completion of a new LP with Tom Petty, Jeff Lynn, and Mike Campbell when he apparently shot himself to death with a .22-

caliber rifle in his home in Santa Clarita on February 8, 1990. It was later learned that Shannon was taking the prescription drug Prozac. Many believe it was the Prozac that altered his mind and caused him to commit suicide.

London

Car Crash Kills Marc Bolan

Driver Gloria Jones Injured

Marc Bolan.

T-REX

Marc Bolan

Steve Peregrine-Took

Born Mark Feld on July 30, 1947, Bolan pursued a modeling career at age fifteen, but his interest soon focused on the pop music world. Originally promoted as Toby Tyler, Bolan soon changed his name to Marc Bowland for his single "The Wizard" and finally settled on the current spelling on his follow-up record, "The Third Degree."

After turning down an offer to play with the Yardbirds, Bolan joined John's Children in 1967. The group had moderate success with their minihit "Desdemona," which was banned on the BBC. After leaving the group, Bolan formed the acoustic duo Tyrannosaurus Rex with Steve Peregrine-Took (Took choked to death in 1980).

By 1970, a transitional period began with the release of the LP *Unicorn*. One side of the LP was acoustic, while the other side was all electric. The LP also included the group's first real hit, "Ride a White Swan," which topped at No. 2 on the U.K. charts.

When Took decided to leave, Mickey Finn was hired to replace him. Bolan shortened the group's name to T-Rex and featured electric instruments on their next release, *Beard of Stars*. The band lineup now included Bolan, Finn, Steve Currie, Bill Legend, and backing vocalists Flo & Eddie (Ex-Turtles Howard Kaylan and Mark Volman).

As the band started producing a string of hits including "Hot

Love," "Get It On (Bang a Gong)," "Telegram Sam," and "Jeepster," the music press referred to T-Rex as the new Beatles. The band was now on top of the charts as a leading British rock group. "New York City," released in 1975, would be the band's last Top 20 hit.

When the band was revamped, the new lineup consisted of Bolan, his girlfriend, Gloria Jones, Dino Dines, and Currie. A short-lived TV series called *Marc* debuted in 1977. The series showcased emerging punk bands. By midyear T-Rex was back on tour with a new lineup that included Bolan, Dines, Herbie Flowers, and Tony Newman. But this, too, would be short-lived.

On September 17, 1977, Bolan was a passenger in a car driven by Gloria Jones when she apparently lost control of the vehicle and hit a tree. Marc Bolan was dead at age thirty. Miss Jones was injured and taken to a hospital. Bolan left behind a infant son he had with Jones.

Ex–Uriah Heep Bassist Found Dead of Overdose

Gary Thain.

URIAH HEEP

Gary Thain

David Byron

Formed in the United Kingdom in 1969, Uriah Heep consisted of Mike Box, David Byron, Alex Napier, Ken Hensley, and Paul Newton. *Very Eavy Very Umble*, released in 1970, featured Hensley's versatile keyboard playing as well as Box's blazing guitar leads. Byron's high-register vocals and the band's outstanding harmonies would take them out of the standard heavy-metal rut. During the recording of the album, drummer Alex Napier left the band. He was replaced by Nigel Olsson, who quit after the recording sessions.

Salisbury, released in 1971, featured new drummer Keith Baker, who had replaced Olsson. The album featured a sixteen-minute title track with heavy orchestration. Keith Baker departed and was replaced by Iain Clarke. Their second release in 1971, *Look at Yourself*, sold well and helped popularize the group. The 1972 release, *Demons and Wizards*, included two more personnel changes. Lee Kerslake replaced Iain Clarke on drums, and Gary Thain replaced Paul Newton on bass.

The album *Magician's Birthday* carried on their wizard-and-sorcery image. *Uriah Heep Live '73* gave the group their first gold record on both sides of the Atlantic. "Easy Livin'," a single release from the live album, earned the group their only Top 40 single. But from there things went downhill. Their 1974 release, *Wonderworld*, did not live up to the band's image, and sales were disappointing. By 1975, personal problems began to show. Gary Thain was constantly arguing with the other band members as his drug habit grew worse. He left the band in 1975 and was found dead on March 19, 1976, from an apparent drug overdose.

During the next year the group had no real direction. Although two albums were recorded, both lacked the energy of their previous albums. This led Byron to leave the band in 1976. On February 19, 1980, founding member David Byron was found dead. He was thirty-three years old.

East Troy, Wisconsin

Plane Crash Kills Blues Legend

Stevie Ray Vaughan.

STEVIE RAY VAUGHAN

Born in Dallas, Texas on October 3, 1954, Stevie Ray Vaughan was heavily influenced by his older brother Jimmie's record collection. By the time Stevie was eight years old, he was already playing in the rock band the Chantones, followed by the band Blackbird.

Dropping out of school to join the Nightcrawlers, Vaughan traveled with the band to Los Angeles to cut an album. The LP was shelved and never released. Between 1975 and 1977, Vaughan played with a popular local band the Cobras before forming his own group, Triple Threat Revue.

Vaughan formed Double Trouble, named after an Otis Rush song, in 1981. The band included ex–Johnny Winter bassist Tommy Shannon and drummer Chris "Whipper" Layton. After receiving rave reviews at the Montreux Jazz Festival in 1982, Vaughan took up Jackson Browne on his offer of some free studio time and in 1983 recorded *Texas Flood*.

During 1983, Vaughan was asked by David Bowie to play lead on his new single "Let's Dance," after which Vaughan started work on his 1984 release, *Couldn't Stand the Weather*. This album paid homage to Jimi Hendrix with the remake of "Voodoo Child." The album also featured Jimmy Reed's "Tin Pan Alley," plus four original songs.

The album *Soul to Soul* followed the same formula with Willie Dixon's "You'll Be Mine." With the addition of keyboard player Reese Wynons, Vaughan's music took on a more modern sound. The band's two-disc live album, *Live Alive*, released in 1986, was considered their best work and established Vaughan as one of the great blues players of our time.

On August 27, 1990, on his way to another concert date, Stevie Ray Vaughan was killed when the plane he was traveling in crashed. Also killed in the crash was Eric Clapton's tour manager, Colin Smythe.

New York

Sid Vicious Found Dead in Greenwich Village Apartment

Sid Vicious.

SID VICIOUS

Born John Simon Richie in London's tough East Side in 1957, Sid Vicious was to become a leading figure in Britain's new punk-rock scene as a member of the Sex Pistols. Vicious "played electric guitar and vomited," according to one music reviewer. He also slashed himself and dripped blood onstage. When asked why he did it, Vicious replied, "To show my disgust at everyone." But these stunts helped make the Sex Pistols the rage of England's alienated youth of the mid-1970s.

After the group broke up in January 1978, Vicious overdosed on a flight from Los Angeles to New York and had to be carried off the plane. After recovering, Vicious moved into the Chelsea Hotel with his girlfriend Nancy Spungen. On October 12, Vicious called the police to report that he awoke that morning to find his girlfriend dead, slumped over the bathroom sink. When police arrived, they discovered that she had been stabbed once in the stomach. Vicious was charged with murder, but was released a few days later on bail.

Soon after his release, Vicious was placed in a psychiatric ward where he slashed his wrists with a broken lightbulb. In December, Vicious was once again arrested, for assault, and was sent to jail for two months.

After completing a detoxification program he was released on February 1, 1979. A party was given in his honor, and guests later said that Vicious seemed to be in good spirits. He drank beer and had a shot of heroin, but seemed fine when everybody left about two A.M. It wasn't until twelve-thirty the next afternoon that he was found lying nude, faceup, on the floor of his apartment. His death was ruled an accidental overdose. Sid Vicious was twenty-one years old.

'50s Rock 'n' Roller Gene Vincent Dead at 36

Gene Vincent (center).

GENE VINCENT

U.S.A. rock 'n' roller of the fifties is the best way to describe Gene Vincent. Born Eugene Vincent in Norfork, Virginia on February 11, 1935, Vincent turned to music after his discharge from the navy. Bill Davis, a local DJ, helped Vincent cut his first demo, "Be-Bop-a-Lula," resulting in Vincent's landing a recording contract with Capitol Records. The song was then recut with the addition of his new band, the Blue Caps. "Be-Bop-a-Lula" was released in 1956 and raced up the charts to reach No. 7 in the United States.

"Race With the Devil" and "Bluejean Bop," his follow-up singles, both failed to chart in the Top 40. The band recorded two more Top 40 hits and became a large live-show attraction before breaking up in 1958. They also appeared in two films, *The Girl Can't Help It* and *Hot Rod Gang*.

Avoiding prosecution by the IRS, Vincent emigrated to the United Kingdom in 1959. Encouraged to promote a rebel image by U.K. pop promoter Jack Good, Vincent soon became Britain's biggest rock-'n'-roll draw. He charted a total of eight Top 40 hits between 1956 and 1961 in the United Kingdom.

Vincent injured his left leg in a motorcycle accident in 1953 and had to wear a brace on his leg thereafter. While on tour in 1960 with Eddie Cochran, he reinjured his leg when the car he was riding in crashed. Eddie Cochran was killed in the accident.

Returning to the United States in 1965, Vincent recorded some country songs for Challenge records. He then returned to the United Kingdom in 1971 in an attempt to rekindle his career, but with little success. On October 12, 1971, Gene Vincent died of a hemorrhaged ulcer.

Miami

Reggae Star Dead of Cancer at 36

Bob Marley (bottom row center).

THE WAILERS

Bob Marley

Peter Tosh

Born in St. Ann's Parish, Jamaica on February 6, 1945, Bob Marley would become Jamaica's first international reggae star.

When Marley was six, his family moved to Kingston, where he grew up in the tough and violent slum known as Trench Town. Influenced by Sam Cooke, Curtis Mayfield, and Brook Benton, Marley started singing and playing in the early sixties, first with Neville Livingston, aka Bunny Wailer, and Peter McIntosh, aka Peter Tosh. Marley formed The Wailers in 1964. Signed to Clement Coxsone Dobbs's Studio One label, the group had a number of local hits. Their first single would sell more than eighty thousand copies.

After the group broke up in 1966, Marley joined his mother, who was living in Delaware, and went to work at the Chrysler plant. Returning to Jamaica to avoid the draft, Marley soon re-formed his group. But brushes with the law and jail time took its toll, and the band split up.

Marley then signed with singer Johnny Nash as a songwriter. He helped Nash develop his unique blend of soul and reggae, and Nash scored with a No. 1 single in the United Kingdom, "Stir It Up."

Marley formed his group again, and it wasn't long before he was signed to Island Records. *Catch a Fire*, released in 1973, was well received by fans and critics alike.

As a political spokesman for the Jamaican masses, Marley

was the target of political gangs. In December 1976, while preparing for a concert, he was shot three times in the arm. He then left for Miami, where he stayed in exile for eighteen months.

Toward the end of his 1980 world tour, Marley collapsed during a performance at New York's Madison Square Garden. His cancer, which Marley had thought was gone after an operation he'd had three years earlier, had spread. He died on May 11, 1981, at Cedars Lebanon Hospital in Miami. Six years later, after looking to re-form the Wailers, Peter Tosh was brutally murdered during an attempted burglary at his home on September 11, 1987. Tosh was forty-two years old at the time of his death.

Los Angeles

Motown Star Mary Wells Dead of Cancer

Mary Wells. (Courtesy Motown Records)

MARY WELLS

As one of the first Motown stars, Mary Wells enjoyed twelve Top 40 hits between 1961 and 1965. "My Guy," written and produced by Smokey Robinson, was Motown's first, and Wells's only, No. 1 single.

Wells started out by singing in local clubs and talent contests in her hometown of Detroit. Auditioning for Motown's Barry Gordy, Wells was immediately signed to the label. Robinson, virtually the only other artist on the label, wrote and produced all but one of her Top 40 singles. Her duets with Marvin Gaye, "Once Upon a Time" and "What's the Matter With You Baby," released in 1964, gave Wells her tenth and eleventh Top 40 singles while recording for Motown.

With the promise of a film contract, which never materialized, Wells left Motown and signed with 20th Century-Fox. Her release of "Use Your Head" on her new label charted at No. 34 and would be her last Top 40 entry on the pop charts. In the years to follow, she continued to chart on the Top 40 soul charts while changing record labels four times.

In August of 1990, Wells was diagnosed with throat cancer. She died on July 26, 1992 at the age of forty-nine.

Los Angeles

Drugs to Blame in Death of Guitarist Danny Whitten

Danny Whitten (standing, left).

DANNY WHITTEN

A founding member of the Los Angeles–based band the Rockets, Whitten, along with Billy Talbot and Ralph Molina, met Neil Young for the first time around 1966. Young, at the time a member of Buffalo Springfield, was recording their debut album.

After recording his first solo LP, Young decided to form a band. He recruited the Rockets and formed the band Crazy Horse. Released in 1969, the album *Everybody Knows This Is Nowhere* is regarded as Young's finest work. In 1970, the band recorded *After the Goldrush*, which would yield Young a No. 1 single called "Heart of Gold." Whitten, now addicted to heroin, was getting hard to handle. Young decided not to use the band on his next album.

Crazy Horse recorded their own LP in 1971, which included Whitten's finest song, "I Don't Want to Talk About It." On November 18, 1972, Danny Whitten died of a heroin overdose. He was twenty-nine years old.

Los Angeles

Alcohol Suspected in Death of Beach Boys' Dennis Wilson

Dennis Wilson.

DENNIS WILSON

With hit songs like "Surfin' USA," "Good Vibrations," and "I Get Around," the Beach Boys created a new sound that would be labeled the California surf sound. The group consisted of three brothers, Brian, Carl, and Dennis Wilson, along with their cousin Mike Love and friend Al Jardin.

In 1960, musician Murry Wilson realized that his sons were his most promising creations. He decided to invest time and money to produce their first record. He also became their manager and immediately began pitching the boys to Capitol Records. This paid off, and soon the Beach Boys had a recording contract with Capitol. Murry Wilson continued to manage the group until 1964, when friction between the boys and him put an end to their professional relationship.

Dennis, being the most physical of the group, was the only member who actually surfed regularly. He would come out of the water and tell Brian what it was really like. Brian then wrote the surfing songs that would make them famous.

On the afternoon of December 28, 1983, Dennis was with friends aboard the yacht *The Emerald* berthed in Marina del Rey. Witnesses stated that Dennis had been swimming, diving, and drinking most of the day. At about four twenty-five P.M. Dennis dived into the water from the slip beside the boat. When he didn't come up, his friends called the harbor patrol and lifeguards. Dennis was found at the bottom, dead. The official report would state that Dennis Wilson had drowned. He was thirty-nine years old

Mount Holly, New Jersey

Jackie Wilson Dies After Eight-Year Coma

Jackie Wilson. (Courtesy Rhino Records)

JACKIE WILSON

Born in Detroit, Michigan, Jackie Wilson sang with local gospel groups and became an amateur boxer before starting his musical career.

Discovered by bandleader Johnny Otis in 1951, Wilson worked as a solo act before replacing Clyde McPhatter as the lead singer in Billy Ward's Dominoes in 1953. Returning to his solo career in 1957, Wilson signed with Brunswick Records. He recorded twenty-four Top 40 pop singles between 1958 and 1968 and over fifty Top 100 entries by 1972. "Lonely Teardrops," released in 1958, reached No. 1 on the R&B charts and was Wilson's first Top 10 entry in the pop charts.

Throughout his career Jackie Wilson was considered one of the most talented and best-loved soul singers of all time. In 1975, the United Kingdom reissued Wilson's 1968 classic, "I Get the Sweetest Feeling," returning Wilson to the top of the charts. But his renewed success was short-lived.

On September 25, 1975, Wilson collapsed onstage at the Latin Casino in Camden, New Jersey, after suffering a heart attack, which led him into an irreversible coma. He remained in a coma until his death, eight years later on January 21, 1984. He was forty-nine years old.

In 1987, Jackie Wilson was inducted into the Rock 'n' Roll Hall of Fame.

London

Traffic's Chris Wood Dead at 39

Chris Wood. (Courtesy Island Records)

CHRIS WOOD

Leaving the Spencer Davis group in 1967, Steve Winwood, together with Chris Wood, Dave Mason, and Jim Capaldi, formed Traffic. After six months of rehearsals in a Berkshire country cottage, Traffic released their first single, "Paper Sun." The single climbed up the British charts to a very respectable No. 5. "Hole in My Shoe," their follow-up release, was even more commercial, rising up the charts to No. 2.

Their first album, *Mr. Fantasy*, revealed the musical talents of each member in the group. A U.S. version of the album was originally called *Heaven Is in Your Mind*. The group also scored another Top 10 single with the sound-track release of "Here We Go Round the Mulberry Bush." By 1968, Traffic had established themselves as a solid force in rock 'n' roll.

Friction between band members caused Mason to leave in December 1967. He returned six months later and contributed four songs to their next album, *Traffic*, before leaving again in October 1968. *Last Exit* was the band's last album of the decade. Soon after its release, in 1969, the group broke up.

Winwood joined Eric Clapton, Ginger Baker, and Rick Grech to form the ill-fated supergroup Blind Faith. After one album the group broke up, and a Traffic reunion album was soon at hand. *Mad Shadows*, which started as a solo album for Winwood, ended up as a group project. The band, still minus Mason, recorded what many feel is their greatest album, *John Barleycorn Must Die*. They successfully combined rock with jazz, folk, and R&B to produce an album unlike any of their others.

Mason once again rejoined the band in 1970. He played only six gigs before departing yet again. Their live album,

Welcome to the Canteen, captured Mason's last appearance with the group.

Departing in December 1971 on a U.S. tour, Traffic won critical acclaim for their release of *The Low Spark of High Heeled Boys*. This was short-lived as Winwood suddenly fell ill and rumors of a breakup began to circulate. After a two-year lull, Traffic released *Shoot Out at the Fantasy Factory* in 1973. They were then off again on a world tour. The live album *On the Road* was recorded during this tour. *Where the Eagle Flies* was recorded in 1974, after which Winwood and Capaldi both pursued solo careers. On July 12, 1983, Chris Wood died of liver failure. He was thirty-nine years old.

Laurel Canyon

Frank Zappa Dead at the Age of 52

Frank Zappa. (Courtesy Starworld)

FRANK ZAPPA

Frank Zappa was born in Baltimore, Maryland, but his family moved to the West Coast when he was a young child. Influenced by R&B, Zappa led his first combo, called the Blackouts, while still in high school. Playing cocktail lounges and writing B-movie scores, Zappa saved enough to purchase a three-track recording studio and began recording various projects.

His next band, the Soul Giants, eventually changed their name to the Mothers and finally to the Mothers of Invention after signing a record deal with Verve Records. Their first album, *Freak-out*, released in 1966, was rock's first two-disc set. And as one of rock's first concept albums, *Freak-out* reached *Billboard*'s Top 200 LPs, establishing Zappa as an important force in rock 'n' roll.

With his bizarre lyrics and often experimental music, Zappa soon developed a large underground following. Titles like "Susie Creamcheese," "Who Are the Brain Police," and "Trouble Every Day" became anthem songs of the counterculture of the mid-1960s. Forming his own record label, Zappa produced and issued Alice Cooper's debut LP along with *Captain Beefheart's Trout Mask Replica*. With his band and as a solo artist, Zappa released nearly sixty albums between 1966 and 1993.

Turning away from rock music after his 1988 world tour lost money, Zappa concentrated on writing classical music. His compositions were performed by the London Symphony Orchestra and the New York Philharmonic, among others.

Diagnosed with prostate cancer around 1990, Zappa vowed not to let the disease conquer him and continued to compose classical pieces as the fatal disease spread. On the evening of Saturday, December 4, 1993, Frank Zappa passed away at his home in Laurel Canyon, California. He was fifty-two years old.

BIBLIOGRAPHY

The Billboard Book of Top 40 Hits
Joel Whitburn
Billboard Publications, 1992

The Penguin Encyclopedia of Popular Music
Viking, 1989

Eight Days a Week
Kenneth Best
Pomegranate Artbooks, 1992

Final Curtain
Everett G. Jarvis
Citadel Press, 1992

The Harmony Illustrated Encyclopedia of Rock
Harmony Books, 1992

Stone Alone
Bill Wyman
Viking, 1990

The Love You Make
Peter Brown and Steven Gaines
McGraw-Hill, 1983

They Went That-a-Way
Malcolm Forbes
Simon & Schuster, 1988

This Day in Rock
John Tobler
Carroll & Graf, 1993

Too Young to Die
Patricia Fox-Sheinwold
Bell Publishing Co., 1982

The Golden Road, 1993 Annual
Blair Jackson

Musician Magazine
BPI Communications

Guitar World Magazine
Harris Publications

Los Angeles Times

New York Times

London Times

Books For Rock Fans
From Carol Publishing Group

Ask for the books listed below at your bookstore. Or to order direct from the publisher call 1-800-447-BOOK (MasterCard or Visa) or send a check or money order for the books purchased (plus $3.50 shipping and handling for the first book ordered and 75¢ for each additional book) to Carol Publishing Group, 120 Enterprise Avenue, Dept. 1581, Secaucus, NJ 07094.

The Art & Music of John Lennon, by John Robertson   paperback $12.95   (#51438)

The Best Rock 'n Roll Records of All Time: A Fan's Guide to the Stuff You Love by Jimmy Guterman   paperback $12.95   (#51325)

Books From Citadel Underground: Classic Books of the Counterculture— Challenging Consensus Reality Since 1990

Bob Dylan: Portraits From the Singer's Early Years by DanielKramer
oversized paperback $16.95   (#51224)

Conversations With the Dead: The Grateful Dead Interview Book by David Gans
paperback $14.95   (#51223)

Death of a Rebel: A Biography of Phil Ochs by Marc Eliot   paperback $14.95   (#51555)

Rock Folk: Portraits From the Rock 'n Roll Pantheon by Michael Lydon; introduction by Peter Guralnick   paperback $9.95 (#51206)

Wanted Man: In Search of Bob Dylan Edited by John Bauldie
paperback $9.95 (#51266)
(call or write for a FREE Citadel Underground brochure)

Dark Star: The Roy Orbison Story by Ellis Amburn   hardcover $18.95   (#40518)

Death by Rock and Roll: The Untimely Deaths of the Legends of Rock by Gary J. Katz
paperwork $9.95   (#51581)

ELVIS! The Last Word by Sandra Choron & Bob Oskam   paperback $ 8.95   (#51280)

The Eric Clapton Scrapbook by Marc Roberty
oversized paperback $16.95   (#51454)

The Howard Stern Book: An Unauthorized, Unabashed, Uncensored Fan's Guide by Jim Cegielski; foreword by "Grampa" Al Lewis
paperback $12.95   (#51505)

The Jimmy Buffett Scrapbook by Mark Humphrey with Harris Lewine
oversized paperback $18.95   (#51461)

The Last Days of John Lennon: A Personal Memoir by Fred Seaman
hardcover $19.95   (#72084)

The Many Lives of Elton John by Susan Crimp & Patricia Burstein   hardcover $19.95 (#72111)

Rock Lyrics Quiz Book by Presley Love
paperback $10.95   (#51527)

Rock Names: From ABBA to ZZ Top—How Rock Bands Got Their Names by Adam Dolgins   paperback $9.95 (#51363)

Rockonomics: The Money Behind the Music by Marc Eliot
paperback $12.95   (#51457)

The Show Must Go On: The Life of Freddie Mercury by Rick Sky
paperback $10.95   (#51506)

Simon & Garfunkel: Old Friends—A Dual Biography by Joseph Morella & Patricia Barey
hardcover $19.95   (#72089)

Sophomore Slumps: Disastrous Second Movies, Albums, Songs and TV Shows by Chris Golden   paperback $14.95   (#51584)

The Worst Rock 'n Roll Records of All Time: A Fan's Guide to the Stuff You Love to Hate by Jimmy Guterman & Owen O'Donnell
paperback $14.95   (#51231)

Prices subject to change; books subject to availability